Marriages Romance And Married Life In Ancient India

(Ancient to Modern)

Marriages Romance And Married Life In Ancient India

(Ancient to Modern)

S. NARAIN

KALPAZ

ISBN: 978-93-5128-252-5

Price: ₹ 590

First Published, 2017

Published by

Kalpaz Publications
C-30, Satyawati Nagar,
Delhi – 110052
E-mail: kalpaz@hotmail.com
Ph.: 9212142040

Printed at: G. Print Process, Delhi

Cataloging in Publication Data—DK
Courtesy: D.K. Agencies (P) Ltd. <docinfo@dkagencies.com>

Narain, S., author.
Marriages romance and married life in ancient India : ancient to modern / S. Narain.
pages cm
ISBN 9789351282525

1. Marriage—India—History. 2. Marriage customs and rites—India—History. I. Title.

HQ669.N37 2016 DDC 306.810954 23

PREFACE

Marriage or vivaha - the most memorable event in the life of a man and woman, celebrated with grandeur and gaity, needs no introduction. In modern India the kinds and options available for marriages, the vivid and colourful ceremonies associated with each kind of marriages and the strange customs followed therein, make an interesting reading.

How the marriage system came in vogue when the people in early days of civilization were hunters and just gatherers of food? How the marriages were celebrated in vedic period and post vedic period? What were the rituals, kind of rides for groom and bride in different periods, the eight kinds of marriage options available to ancients is really a fanciful and enjoyable account. The art of making love, romance in ancient India will refresh any body besides the premarital and extra-martial sex in practice in those days.

I hope the book will prove interesting to the married couples and those who are getting married and also to the lover of Ancient India.

S. Narain

CONTENTS

1

Modern Weddings Vs Grandeur & Gaiety

1

MODERN WEDDINGS VS GRANDEUR AND GAIETY

Weddings are grand affairs in India – an index to showcase the riches, wealth and resources of the person hosting a wedding. No stone is left unturned to make the occasion as pompous and glamorous as possible. The eminent political personalities, the celebrities of various walks of life, may it be

Fig. 1 :

Fig. 2 : *One of the costliest palaces of UK where the post wedding ritual of L.N. Mittal's daughter was held.*

film or dance or literature, senior beaurocrates, all efforts are made to bring them to the wedding venue.

An Indian wedding is no doubt a unique experience – fascinating confluence of colour and celebration, glitter and gold, décor, dinning & dancing. From selecting the shubh mahurat & the right venue, to shop for trousseau, searing for appropriate invitation card, the list appears endless.

Fig. 3 : *A luxirous cruiser is also used as venue of wedding.*

There have been grand and ostentatious marriages in the recent times. The great steel tycoon of the world L.N. Mittal a NRI and the richest man of U.K. spent a whooping amount over 250 crores of rupees in the marriage of his daughter - a world record in expensive marriages. More advanced, funny and wealthier persons have gone a step further to celebrate marriages in special aeroplanes and in luxirous cruiser sailing in deep sea.

A Cosy Marriage of Rs. 100/- Crores at Jaipur

10 Crores Hospitality & Entertainment	**9 Crores** Bridal Make-up & Jewellery	**3 Crores** Marriage venue	**10 Crores** Miscellaneous Expenditure for Marriage
3 Crores Performance Stage	**6 Crores** Costume Design	**1 Crore** Invitation Cards	**15-20 Crores** Return Gift

A history of grandeur and gaiety of costliest marriage was created at Jaipur-the pink city of India recently, where the money was flowing like water in hiring the costliest Pop singer of the world, Ricky Martin of the time who was presented a golden set of Rs. 1 Crore. The marriage was held between Kanika- the daughter of an industrialist and the son of Neeraj Raja Kachar another industerialist of Mumbai. All the celebraties of film world, industries, political big boss lined up at the occasion. A special dome like scene was created in La-Meridian Hotel at Jaipur where the world famous Pop singer presented his performance and enthralling the participants. A herd of elephants and camels was also stealing the show.

A MARRIAGE OF POMP SHOW AND SPICE[1]
(Liz-Nayar Wedding)

Umaid Bhawan

1.7 Crores	**4.4 Crores**	**9 Private**	**7 Lakh**
Spent on various ceremonies	Hotel Rent 125 luxury tents.	Jets for guests.	Diamond set for Liz.

Jodhpur - the Blue City of India witnessed a grand affair of marriage held between Liz Hurley - a super model & actress of Hollywood & Arun Nayar - a NRI based at London. Liz has already a son of four years in her lap from her earlier husband & now desires to have more children on her union with Nayar. The marriage was unique in many respects, as the same couple has undergone two marriages, one at a church in U.K. solemnized in Christian tradition & the second leg was held at Umaid Bhawan Palace of Jodhpur in accordance with Hindu tradition. An estimated amount of Thirteen Crores of Rupees was spent on all the ceremonies including over One Crore on hospitality, which was met by London tabloid, which bagged exclusive media rights for the events.

Of course, all the traditions leading up to the marriage were filmy to the T. To begin with there was the *mehendi ceremony,* for which specialist Veena Nagda was flown in from Mumbai. Liz got a *dulha* designed on her hand and an elephant on her right. She also requested for the name 'Arun' to be inscribed on her ring finger. And Arun asked for a large 'E' to be inscribed on his palm, as Liz preferred to be called Elizebeth and not 'Liz'. The event saw Liz wearing a *red saree* and stunning emerald and ruby jewellery traditionally set - a gift from her mother-in-law. Arun wore an orange *sherwani* and Liz's four-year-old son Damian looked cute in a sherwani too. For the wedding ceremony, Umaid Bhawan Palace was decked up with flowers and illuminated, while Rajasthani folk musicians provided the rustic charm. The reception in Mehrangarh Fort was made interesting by the fact that both Liz and Arun were carried there in a specially - made *palkhi.*

The groom, on horse-back, wore a white-and-gold Rohit Bal outfit and the bride a Versace. We're talking about Elizabeth Hurlery and Arun Nayar's big fat Indian 'shaadi' at Jodhpur's majestic Umaid Bhawan Palace.

Liz, graceful in her pink out-fit, was the perfect bride.

Walking into the courtyard next to the ballroom at Umaid Bhawan Palace, one could see the elegantly done up mandap area decorated with traditional marigolds. A *havan kund* was placed in the centre. Liz and her leading man could take only four *pheras* around the sacred fire as their clothes kept getting entangled. The moment, nevertheless, was an emotional one - there was not a dry eye in the area. Following the traditional nuptials, the guests celebrated with champagne and canapes.

The wedding party subsequently moved to the subtly-lit Meherangarh Fort, where a sit-down meal and DJ Aqeel awaited them. Cocktail snacks, including the local favourite lamb bootha, were served along with accompanying wines. For dinner, there was the royal Rajasthani thali with two non-veg and three vegetarian dishes. DJ Aqeel then took over and made everybody dance to his tunes. Disco, house and a bit of Bollywood was the flavour of the night. Popular

Liz as bride

Liz in a fashion show with a gown of 6.43 Lakhs

among the Hindi hits were *Dus Bahane* and *Where's The Party Tonight*, that had Pretty flashing her gorgeous dimples.

The Meherangarh Fort

THE MOST SPECTACULAR AND EXPENSIVE MARRIAGE IN CLOSE RESONANCE WITH ANCIENT HINDUISM[3] :

Hollywood's most expensive and spectacular marriage reported in almost various news channels worldwide was held recently (Nov. 2006) in a small town of Italy between Tom Cruise and Katt Holmes – the top film stars of Hollywood. Over one lakh of people participated/attended the wedding ceremony. One of the news channels of Italy spent around 40 lakhs Dollars to cover the event through satellite. There was direct telecast

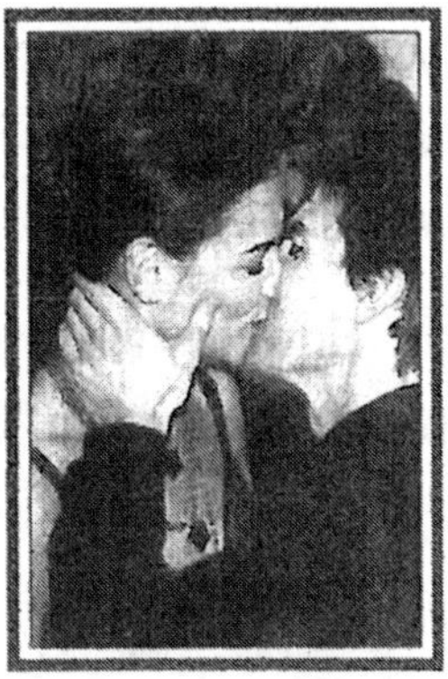

of the ceremony. The news channels of U.K., USA & other countries procured the CD of the event and telecast it worldover and an estimated amount worth around 20 million dollars is believed to have been spent on the marriage.

What is more remarkable is that the celebration of the marriage has close similarity between Tom Cruise's religion scientology and the oldest living faith on earth – the Hinduism which mentions eight kinds of marriages, however, under scientology, there are 5 options of marriage. With vows of duties, respect, love and fidelity, similar to that we have under the ritual of Satpadi.

A BIG AND FAT WEDDING OF BOLLYWOOD

The wedding of Abhishek and Aishwarya Rai hogged the headlines of News Media world wide. Abhishek is the son

of "Big B" and a top ranking actor of Bollywood and Aishwarya Rai is Miss World regarded as the most beautiful woman and also a top-actoress, the Neptunian knot recently in the month of April,2007 and has been the most talked about wedding event.

How they fell in has an interesting story. They both were together in the film "Dhaii Aákshar Prem ka" with romantic roles. After the shooting of the film, Abhishek Bachchon proposed Aish "would you marry me?" which she accepted and said Yes! Then began the horoscopic matching after both the family consented. Aishwarya was found to be *Manglik* which is considered as *Dosha* from marriage point of view under the *Hindu Faith.*

To ward off ill-effects, there are rituals that almost every *Manglik* girl endures, like special pujas, wearing specific gemstones, reciting the *Hanuman Chalisa* or *Ganesha mantra* and visiting temples.

Visit to Tirupati Shrine

At Vindhya Vasini Shrine

SANGEET CEREMONY

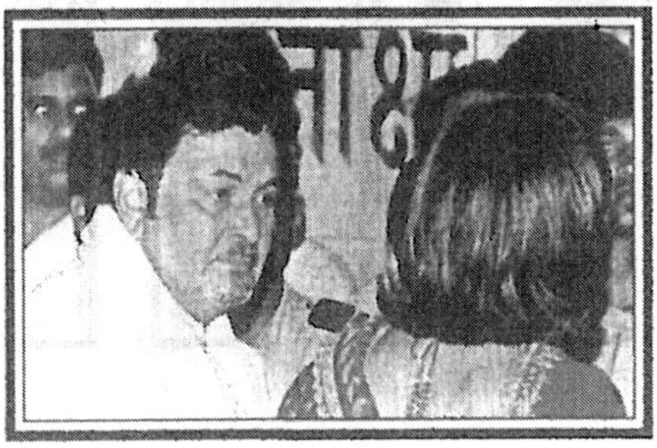

Celebrities floacking to Sangeet Ceremony

The pre-marriage proceeds kicked off from sangeet ceremony attended by celebrities from all walks of life.

The *sangeet* began with a soft Indian dance performance and as the momentum built up, it went from *dhin-chak* to hot modern numbers. "Big B and Jaya did some cool moves". There were about 11 songs in this programme. Aishwarya and her family member also put up a performance". The *sangeet* was bigger than the *shaadi* in the Bachchan family.

The Bachchans danced in the half-hour *sangeet ceremony* at Prateeksha. The groom's sister Shweta was also a part of the dancing. "Every-one from Amitabh to Shweta's son Agastaya danced in the *sangeet* with every top actor's song, right from SRK, Salman etc.

A GRAND WEDDING - HIGH LIGHTS

Abhishek as groom

Aishwarya as bride

BRIDAL SAREES
An exquisite hand-woven sambalpuri saree for the bride and two Sonepuri 'Paat' (Silk) Sarees 'Double 'Ikat' and Radhakunja'- cost Rs. 2.30 lakh.

SINDOOR
The Sindoor was brought from a Vindyachal

VOLVO BARAAT
SEVEN VOLVO buses for the wedding.

MENU
Chefs from Mumbai, Delhi, Banglore, Kolkata and Hyderabad. Best of delicacies from India, Continental, Mexican, Thai and Chinese Cuisines.

As the most eligible bachelor of the country, Abhishek Bachchan, wed the most beautiful woman in the world, Aishwarya Rai, the quiet Juhu neighbourhood saw frenzied activity. A burst of flaming gilmohurs and bright bougainvillea formed a colourful canopy over the two wedding venues – Jalsa and Prateeksha, the two Bachchan bunglows located within a five-minute drive each other and staked out with scores of security guards and policemen.

A whoop of joy went up in the summer air as the bridegroom's party emerged from Jalsa a few minutes before 5 pm. But onlookers, especially mediapersons were disappointed when the fleet of massive luxury Konduskar buses hired by the Bachchans to ferry wedding guests to and fro moved in to conceal the view.

Marriage Procession

But even the Konduskars and sehra (veil) of fragrant white jasmine could not mask Abhishek's excitement as he rode out on a white mare. As the wedding band struck the opening notes of the couple's song Kajra Re, the young actor raised a hand to greet the crowd and obliged them with a little shoulder jig that sent them into ecstasy- and made all that waiting worth it. Within minutes, however, Abhishek dismounted and boarded one of the buses that headed for Prateeksha, where the wedding ceremony was later performed.

Not invited but there in full force were fans. They had clambered on to tall trees and commandeered rooftops of neighboring buildings, grabbing every vantage point they possibly could to get a dekko.

Dressed in a rich, maroon Kanjeevaram, Aishwarya arrived from LA Meridian to Prateeksha at about 2.25pm in a gray Mercedes Benz decorated with red and white flowers. Her parents, Vrinda and Krishnaraju Rai, kept a low profile. So did Jaya Bachchan. Papa Bachchan however, was seen shouting instruction to band mem-

Local People clambered on trees to get a glimpse of Marriage Procesion

bers for blocking the way of the buses ferrying guests from Jalsa.

Outside the gates of Prateeksha, Abhishek and nephew Agastya mounted a horse surrounded by dancing baraatis, who all wore mango-coloured safas. Among them were industrialist and family friend Anil Ambani with wife Tina, film maker Karan Johar, actor Ajay Devgan, Riteish Deshmukh, Dimple Kapadia and producer Goldie Behl and wife Sonali.

As the Barat entered the house, Abhishek, dressed in a heavily embroidered Abu-Sandeep sherwani, briefly waved to the hysterical crowd sending media hounds and zealous fans in frezy. But once inside, the large, wooden gates to landmark bungalow were closed.

The ceremony kicked off at 6.13pm with an exchange of garlands. Eleven pandits chanted sacred mantras under the guidance of Chandramouli Upadhyay, a member of the Kashi Vishwanath Mandir Trust. It ended at around 8 pm with a big feast with chefs from the Taj groups serving India, Thai, Chinese and Continental fare.

The party then returned to Jalsa where the celebrations continued. Late in the night, Aishwarya moved back to La Meridian for the bidaai ceremony, which was scheduled to take place early next day. The couple visited the Balaji Temple in Tirupati on the following day and then left for a honeymoon in Venice.

REFERENCES :

1. News Reporting, Punjab Kesari, 4 Feb. 2007
2. News Reporting, T.O.I., 10 March 07
3. News Report, T.O.I., 20 & 21 April, 07
4. News Report, H.T., 20 & 21 April, 07

2

Modern Weddings Ceremonies & Options

2

MODERN WEDDINGS CEREMONIES & OPTIONS

India- a country of diverse culture, creed and faith, the rituals of marriage differ considerably depending upon the faith and religion being practiced by the wedding couple. Here, we have Hindu wedding, Sikh wedding, Bengali wedding, Buddhist wedding, Parsi wedding, etc. The customs, tradition and the concept in each case are at variance accordingly. The local traditions, language, geographical conditions also play an important role in defining the ceremonies of a marriage largely.

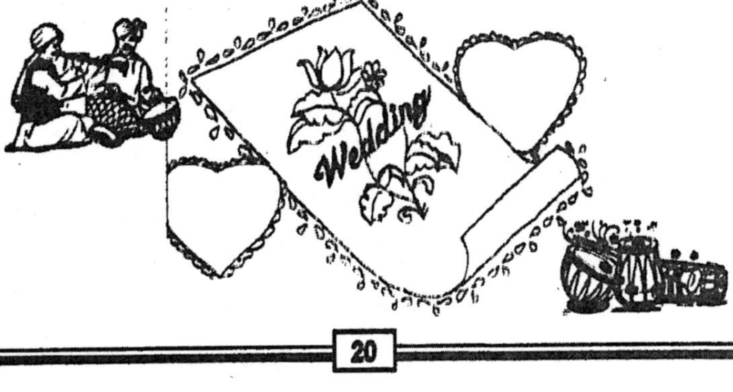

Hindu Weddings

वक्रतुण्ड महाकाय, सूर्य कोटी समप्रभः ।
निर्विघ्नं कुरुमे देव, सर्वकार्येषु सर्वदाः ।।

Hinduism which is the most ancient faith on earth regards the wedding as a religious affair-a union of two souls for procreation and fulfillment of spiritual obligation to God. Through the ritual of satpadi, the bride and groom take vows of duty, love, respect and fidelity and companionship for all stages to traverse the mundane journey of life through fair or foul weather, ups and down, happiness and sorrow with holy fire God as witness. They make themselves accountable to the creator of the universe to adhere to the vows taken by them.

In Hindu weddings the parents of the bride search for a suitable groom through social contact or advertisements in newspaper and selection is done with sole regard to the interest of their daughter and compatibility. The ultimate choice is, however, left to 'would be bride' as well as groom and meeting is arranged to enable each other to see and to talk to each other to get their consent. Date of marriage is fixed from astrological consideration. Also matching of horoscope is got done some times for finalising the selection of groom. For marriage relationship blood relations, Gotras and close relations are avoided.

SAGAN OR TILAK CEREMONY

As per Hindu tradition, marriage proceedings are initiated by mangni or roka where the would be bride & groom exchange rings along with give & take of sweets, dry fruits and some gifts between the two families.

However, the pre-wedding ceremony starts from 'Sagan' or 'Tilak' ritual which is held few days before the wedding. This symbolizes confirmation or the acceptantce of groom by

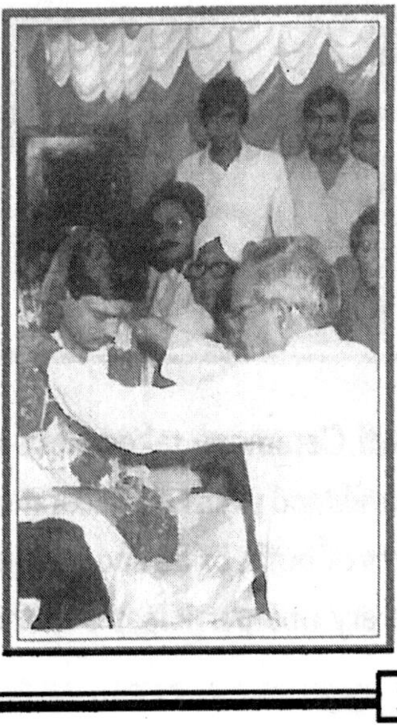

the family of the bride. The groom seated on dias with family members and relatives of both sides around him performs brief pooja with recitations of mantaras by a pandit praying Lord Ganesha to remove any problem or obstacle in the performance of the ceremony. The bride's father thereafter garlands the groom and apply 'tilak' on his forehead and give lavish gifts like gold chain, wrist watch, wedding suit and other souvenirs. On their part groom's close relatives present the bride with some dresses and ornaments as a mark of accepting her into their family. As per recent trend, the mother and sisters of the groom dress up the bride, apply bindi and put 'sindur' in her hairs and take her in their lap symbolizing their affection and her acceptability. The other ladies of the family present cash as a gift to the bride. The later part of the ceremony is called 'God Bharai' means taking the bride into lap. Then follows lavish hospitality by the father of the bride.

Ladies Sangeet and Mehndi Ceremony takes place a day before the wedding. Brides hands and palms are decorated with Mehndi. Friends & relatives of both, bride and groom get their hands hennaed and every one participates in the dance and music with full fervor making it a very joyous and festive event.

Morning of the wedding day sees the Batna ceremony wherein gram flour mixed with mustard oil is applied on the body of bride and groom followed by thorough bath to get ready for the big occasion in the evening.

The Barat with the groom astride a horse proceeds to the wedding venue, accompanied by fire works, dancing and music. On reaching the venue, the bride's family receives the groom and procession by exchanging garlands with their counterparts. After Milni, the groom is welcomed by Bhabhi's & sisters of the bride.

The exchange of garlands takes place between the bride and the groom atop a bedecked stage after which they proceed for the real ceremony of nuptial knot on taking specially prepared meal by the host.

MANDAP & SAPT PADI (SAAT PHERE) :

This is the most important ritual of the marriage. A special Mandap is prepared and tastefully decorated. The close family members of both sides and close relatives are supposed to participate in the ceremony. The father-mother of the bride & groom are normally present. Fire altar is prepared by Pandits & worship is made invoking all Gods and thereafter fire is ignited.

The bride and groom seated together are tied through knot by joining their shawls and take seven steps around the fire altar amidst the chanting of Mantras by Pandits and given seven vows to be abided by them after marriage.

VOWS FOR GROOMS[1] :

- That Yajnas under religious events will be performed with mutual consent and participation.
- That any act of charity and philanthropy will carry her (Wife) consent.
- The 3rd vow seeks respect, love, food and clothing etc. under all circumstances and in all three stages of her life i.e. adolescent, middle and old age.

- That the groom will consult her in all the matters relating to wealth, property and money etc.
- That he will look after her in all weathers, seasons and every where.
- That no insulting or harsh words will be so spoken by him before her friends, relatives etc.

VOWS FOR BRIDES[2] :

This time the gifts start pouring in

- That she will follow creed and faith of her husband & his family too.
- That she will care for the comfort of the family of the groom and speak, sweet and soft wordings free from anger, irritation or laziness.
- That she will follow good advice conforming to Dharma of elders of the groom and his family.
- That she will give honour and good name to her husband.
- That she will be obedient to her husband.

With the exchange of these vows the marriage relationship is established. In the end, there is prayer for the well being not only for both the families but also for the whole world.

A high philosophy is yoked to the ritual of 'Satpadi'. By taking seven steps together around the altar and taking oath separately in presence of holy and divine fire God, the bride and groom are bound to associate with each other in fair and foul weather, in ups and downs of life and in discharge of religious, social duties and obligations and are accountable to the creaters of universe in case of default in any respect.

KANYA DAAN

In Hinduism, bride is given away to the groom as a free gift or charity – daan and hence the ritual is called Kanya daan.

It amounts to a great sacrifice on the part of the father of the bride who loses the useful services of a member of the family and also doing a heavy expenditure in holding the marriage ceremony for noble cause to enable the continuing of the human race by procreation through the marriage as 'kanya daan' is regarded as Maha daan i.e. a great charity free from any selfish motive.

The ritual of Kanya daan is performed before satpadi. The father of the bride pours a libation of pure water or Ganga water symbolizing love for the bride and the groom with the following pronouncement –

"I hearby give my daughter with all the virtues and embodiment of goddess of wealth and prosperity (Lakshmi) to you (groom) the embodiment of lord Vishnu for dharma, artha, kama, moksha i.e. fulfillment of religious obligation prosperity, wealth, procreation enjoyment and salvation."

Parents on both sides now bless the couple for a Happy and Prosperous Life. Other guests also greet and bless the Newly Weds.

After the sumptuous meal, Baraat is ready to leave with the bride. While leaving her home to start a new life in the new abode, the relatives of the bride bid her a tearful farewell.

When the doli reaches the groom's house, it is welcomed by groom's mother.

In Indian context wedding is not just a union of two souls but between two families.

Bengali Wedding

Introduction

A Bengali marriage is also basically a Hindu Marriage. However terms used for various ceremonies are adapted as per Bengali culture and lanugage. The Satpadi ritual is called 'Saat Paak' & Varmala is called 'Malabadal'.

Welcoming the Groom

Wedding Ceremony Starts when the marriage procession of the groom arrives at the doorsteps of the bride's residence. They are greeted with fresh flowers. An elderly female relative of the bride holds the baran dala. The plate is firstly touched to the groom's forehead, then to the ground. Thereafter, it is touched back again to his forehead. This gesture symbolizes part blessing. After that, the groom is given sweets and sharbat. As the groom enters the bride's house, rose water is sprinkled on him.

Shubho Drishti Ritual

In this ritual, the bride and groom see each other.

Mala Badal Ceremony

Mala badal ceremony involves the exchange of flower garlands between the bridge and groom while the purohit chants mantras.

Saat Paak & Sampradhan

As a part of Saat Paak ritual, the bride is made to sit on a low wooden stool called pidi that is lifted by her brothers. Thereafter, the girl is taken around the groom in circles seven times. It signifies their union. In the Sampradhan ritual, the bride is given away to the groom by her paternal or maternal uncle. Thereafter, saptapadi ritual takes place.

A Sikh Wedding

Sikhism[3] regards marriage a blissful union of two individuals joined in equal partnership.

According to the official Sikh Code of conduct, no thought should be given to the perspective spouses caste, race or lineage. As long as both the boy and girl profess the Sikh faith and no other faith they may be joined in wedlock by the Anand Karaj ceremony. The Reht Maryada strictly forbids any sort of dowry arrangement as marriage is not to be viewed as a business transaction. Sikhs are also discouraged from consulting horoscopes or following any other superstitions pertaining to determining a wedding date or time. The Anand Karaj ceremony can be performed in any Gurdwara or home where Sir Guru Granth Sahib has been respectfully installed. The religious ceremony cannot be performed in a hotel or banquet hall. There are no restrictions as to what time the ceremony should start or what time it should end although they are usually performed in the morning with the religious ceremony taking not more than a few hours.

Marriages are normally one or two day's affair. Either the wedding occurs in the morning followed by a dinner and dance in a banquet hall or hotel at night, or the religious ceremony and banquet takes place on consecutive days. In some cases only the religious ceremony takes place.

READING OF THE LAVANS

The religious ceremony can be conducted by any respected Sikh man or woman. In case it is being conducted by the local Granthi who is incharge of respectfully looking after Sri Guru Granth Sahib, the ceremony officially begins after having ascertained that both the bride and groom are Sikhs, asking the couple as well as their parents to stand up for Ardas. This family Ardas indicate the public consent of the parties involved to this marriage taking place. Every time the bride and groom arise or sit down during the ceremony they will bow down

to Sri Guru Granth Sahib out of respect by touching their foreheads to the ground. After Ardas the couple sit down and the officiate then lectures the couple on the significance of marriage, their duties and obligations to each others as equal partners. The couple indicate their agreement to these guidelines and principles by bowing down before Sri Guru Granth Sahib. The father of the bride then places one end of a scarf or sash worn by the groom over his shoulders in his daughter's hand signifying that she is now leaving his care to join her husband. The officiate now reads the Lavan hymn of Guru Ram Das which is composed of four stanzas. The four stanzas of the hymn describe the progression of love between a husband and wife which is analogous to that between the soul (bride) and God (the husband). After the conclusion of the recitation of each stanza, the groom followed by the bride holding the end of the scarf go around Sri Guru Granth Sahib in a clockwise direction while the ragis sing out the recited Lavan stanza. After each round the couple sit down and listen while the officiate reads the next stanza. The ragis then sing it while the

Lavan Reading

couple completes another walk around Sri Guru Granth Sahib. This process is repeated four times in total for each stanza of the Lavan, after which the couple sit down. During their walk around Sri Guru Granth Sahib often there are members of the girls family who help her complete her rounds with her husband. This is to signify their support for her as she leaves one family for another.

CONCLUSION OF THE RELIGIOUS FUNCTION

After the Lavan, the Anand hymn by Guru Amar Das is recited. This is followed by lectures and kirtan. The religious ceremony is formally concluded by the entire congregation standing for the final Ardas of the marriage. After this Sri Guru Granth Sahib is now opened to any page at random and the hymn is read out as the days order from the Guru for the

Final Ardas

occasion (hukamnama). Karah Prashad, ceremonial sacramental pudding is then distributed to everyone to mark the formal conclusion of the ceremony.

Muslim Marriage

٧٨٦

शादी खाना आबादी

Marriage[3] is a civil union for fulfillment of sexual urge and pro-creation of sons according to Muslim religion, which allows up to four wives for the purpose regarded as status symbol also. The husband enjoys a dominating power on property matters and almost absolute power to divorce, which is so simple that uttering *'Talak'* three times would tentamount to final divorce.

It is the man who makes a purposal to a women for her hand in marriage or for that matter to her family. Islam considers it as an act of respectability and dignity for woman.

There are certain blood relations which are considered as haraam (for bidden) as far as marriages are concerned.

For Man : Mother, daughter, paternal aunt, maternal aunt, niece, foster-mother, foster-sister, mother-in-law, stepdaughter, daughter-in-law, all married women, sister-in-law (as a 2nd Wife) (see the Qur'an, Ch. 4, verse 23-24).

For Woman : Father, son, paternal uncle, maternal uncle, nephew, foster-mother's husband, foster-brother, father-in-law, stepson, son-in-law.

Mahr : The intending husband is asked to offer a Mehr (free gift) to the bride which is settled in advance by the marriage partners. The Mehr may be in cash in hand or in form of services (like training) etc.

HARAAM ACTS :

Some of the rituals in marriage ceremonies are absolutely Haraam like the playing of music. It is also Haraam for ladies to go for mixed gatherings without proper Hijab. Such things invite divine wrath and take away the blessings of this auspicious occasion. In the Islamic Law, marriage is an Aqd, a contract.

THE NIKAH CEREMONY :

This is the most important ceremony and the marriage is regarded as complete thereby. The marriage partners are asked to recite the following formula in Arabic.

According to Shariah, the wife-to-be says, 'An Kah'tu nafsaka a'lal mah'ril ma'loom'. ("I have given away myself in Nikah to you, on the agreed Mahr").

Immediately, the man (bridegroom) says, 'Qabiltun Nikaha'. ("I have accepted the Nikah").

With these pronouncements, they become husband and wife. If the marrying partners are not able to recite the formula in Arabic, one or two persons or priests are appointed and authorized to officiate to make the appropriate pronouncement.

In Muslim marriages, husbands may have up to four wives which is traditionally considered to be a sign of status among Muslim communities. Muslim women do not have rights to own anything which is a matter of culture and as well as religion.

VALIMA (DINNER) :

Valima is highly recommended for the groom. The relatives, neighbours and friends must be invited for Valima. However, lavish spending is not advisable especially when the same money can be used effectively by the couple.

THE WEDDING NIGHT :

It is highly recommended that the wedding should take place at night. The hadith says, "Take the bride to her new home during the night". When the bride enters the room, the groom is recommended to take off her shoes and wash her feet (in a washbowl) and then sprinkle the water around the room. Then he should perform wuzu and pray two-rak'at sunnat prayer.

Christian Marriages (Ethopian)

In[3] arranged Christian marriages, groom's parents search for a bride for their son and then terms of the marriage are set through a mediator and then parents of both sides meet at a mutually convenient date and location. It is important that the families on the both sides are not related by blood for the last five generations.

When the parents have reached an agreement, the man and woman get engaged. The parents then set a wedding date and they meet all the wedding expenses. The bride and groom first see each other on their wedding day. Both parents prepare food and drink for the wedding and invite guests. The groom goes to the bride's house to take his wife to be. The wedding ceremony starts with dance and music and the bride's parents give the groom a dowry, in most cases, of money and cattle. At the end of the ceremony the groom takes his bride to his parents' house. The groom takes the bride's virginity during the first three days after the marriage. The honeymoon will last between one week to three months dependant on the groom's parents' economic circumstances. This takes place at the husband's parents' house and often the best man/men will also be present. After the honeymoon the couple return to the house of the bride's parents where they stay together for a set time, again with the best man/men present. During the honeymoon, the bride is not allowed to go out during the day; she is only allowed to go out after sunset.

Nowadays, many men and women, often those, who live in urban areas do not follow this tradition and do not have arranged marriages but it is important to marry someone the family approves of.

ROMAN CATHOLIC CHRISTIAN MARRIAGE[4]

A Catholic priest prepares to administer the sacrament of communion to a wedding couple. (above)

"Only those marriages are valid that are celebrated with a sacred rite, in the presence of the local hierarch, local pastor, or a priest who has been given the faculty of blessing the marriage by either of them, and at least two witnesses ...

Parsi Wedding

The marriage[3] starts with 'Madhavsaro' ritual which is celebrated four days before the lagan. The families of the bride and groom each plant a young tree in a pot, amidst recitation of prayers by the family priest, and place this at the entrance of their homes. This is generally a mango plant and is treated as a symbol of fertility. The plant is watered every morning till the eighth day after the wedding and then transplanted elsewhere.

Adarni on the third day before the lagan, is celebrated as a day for gift exchanging. On this day, the groom's family visits the bride's home to present her with all kinds of gifts like clothes, jewellery etc.

This ritual of gifting the bride is known as Adarni. The relatives, neighbours and friends are invited for a traditional meal of sev and dahi, boiled eggs and bananas. The day before the wedding is called Supra nu Murat. It is more like the mehendi and haldi ceremony of the Hindus. In this ritual four married women are given a supra each, containing paan, supari, haldi, dates and a piece of coconut. While singing traditional songs, these supras are exchanged seven times among the women cross-wise, length-wise and breadth-wise. A fifth lady sits in the middle with a khalbatto and dry turmeric. Then a paste of it is applied by all to the groom and bride along with a showering of blessings.

WEDDING DAY RITUALS

The bride madhavate the white, ornate wedding saree given by her parents, while he groom wears the traditional Parsi dagli and feta - a white kurta like garment and a black cap. The Parsi lagan is called Achumichu, which takes place either at a baug or at an agiary (the fire temple). A stage is builts up for the couple and before they step on it, the groom first, a ritual called achumichu is performed. The bride's mother takes a tray with a raw egg, supari, rice, coconut, dates and water and begins the ceremony with her son-in-law to be. In Ara antar ceremony the couple is made to sit facing each other with a cloth held between them, so they cannot see the other. Among the other main day rituals are Chero bandhvanu, Haath borvanu, etc.

The next day reception is held in a grand manner with varied menu of food, drink and music. The menu mainly comprises of traditional Parsi dishes like Parsi bhonu like sarya (crisps), (achaar – rotli (pickle and rotis), patra ni macchi (steamed fish), salli margi (chicken with potato crisps), lagan nu custard, pulao-dal and ice cream. The wedding ceremony ends with the couple being accompanied home by the bride's family and the achumichu being performed once again by the groom's mother for the well being of the couple.

Buddhist Wedding

In Buddhism, marriage is considered as personal and individual concern, and not as a **religious** duty. Buddhism does not compel a person to be married. It does not force somebody to remain as a bachelor.

The parties take a blessing from monks at the local temple after the civil registration formalities have been completed. Although Buddhist monks do not solemnize a marriage ceremony, they do perform religious services in order to bless the couple. From the Buddhist point of view, marriage is neither holy nor unholy. Buddhism does not regard marriage as a religious duty nor as a sacrament that is ordained in heaven.

MATCHMAKING

The matchmaking is usually done by taking the boy and the girl in confidence. It could be by the parents of either side or by the eligible boy himself. When the boy finds a suitable girl for him, he would usually send a family friend to the girl's house. The friend would generally carry a wine bottle or any other alcohol bottle for that matter. Additionally he carries a white silk scarf - khada.

COSTUMES

Bridal Wear :

The Buddhist bride has this dress made of brocade called Bhaku. The dress resembles a sarong, only it has to be full length. The bride wears it with a sleeved blouse, Hanju. The Hanju is usually made of Chinese silk called khichen. She also wears a special coat and a scarf. Some unusual jewellery (Khau) is also worn by her which are made of large precious and semi-precious stones for example turquoise, coral, pearl, etc

Groom's Attire :

A Buddhist groom also wears a Bhaku, one that is with sleeves. The bhaku reaches to just above the ankles. The bhaku looks beautiful as it is made of brocade and is worn with a waistcoat called Lajha. The boy would also wear a cap, also made of brocade and a sash around the waist.

Nangchang

This is the ceremony which has the formal engagement taking place. The Nangchang is presided over by a lama or rimpoche. The maternal uncles of both the sides play an important role in the ongoing marriage negotiations. On the boy's side, the mama and the siblings play important role. Whereas, the girl's side has the entire family, friends and the mama joining the occasion. The guests would bring Tsang and many kinds of meat to the girl's house. They gift rice and chicken especially to the girl's mother. This is a token payment for the mother to have breast-fed her girl. The ritual has that the meat and tsang are also given to the girl's mamas as well as to the unmarried elder sisters and brothers. The kikas would be matched again and an auspicious date for the marriage is fixed. A propitious day is also decided for the girl's departure from her maiden house. The young couple mostly live together either in the girl's or the boy's house after the engagement.

Marriage Rituals

Following are a set of fundamental rituals that commonly feature in Buddhist marriage:-

- In front of the shrine of Lord Buddha all set up with candles and flowers, the to-be married couple, the family and the guests would collect. The boy and the girl and others would recite the Tisarana, Pancasila and the Vandana in either English or Pali.
- The boy and the girl are asked to light the candles and incense sticks. Then they offer flowers to the image of Buddha and around it.
- After this the bride and the groom must recite in turn, the vows that are prescribed for each of them in the Sigilovdda

Sutta (Digha Nikilya): **Vow for the groom:** "Towards my wife I undertake to love and respect her, be kind and considerate, be faithful, delegate domestic management, provide gifts to please her." **Vow for the bride:** "Towards my husband I undertake to perform my household duties efficiently, be hospitable to my in-laws and friends of my husband, be faithful, protect and invest our earnings, discharge my responsibilities lovingly and conscientiously."

- At the end, only the parents or the assembly would recite the Mangala Sutta and Jayamangala Gatha to offer their blessings for the couple.

As for the Vidaai (girl's leaving maiden house for husband's house) ceremony, it is quite common for the newly wed couple to opt to stay at the girl's house. They could also decide to stay separately from either family.

Rituals After Marriage

The girl's departure from her paternal house is also selected from the kika. This day could be any day between the first day after marriage till the tenth day.

SOME STRANGE CUSTOMS

Buddhist marriage is quite a boisterous affair, wherein the boy's family arrives at the girl's place. The custom has it that a pot of water, flowers, bamboo sticks are arranged in a typical way and leaves adorn the entrance for good luck. The girl's sisters welcome the boy and his friends in a rather prickly way. They throw nettle leaves and thorns etc on them. It is done because they want the groom to give them some suitable presents or money. Till then the groom would not be allowed to enter the hall.

After the blessing, the couple and guests would usually go to a reception. As there are no hard-and-fast marriage traditions in the Buddhist faith, what happens next is entirely up to the couple.

REFERENCES

1. कन्यायाः सप्त वाक्यानि
    1. यदि यज्ञं कुर्यात्तस्मिन्मम सम्मतिं गृह्णीयात्।
    2. यदि दानं कुर्यात्तस्मिन्नपि मम सम्मतिं गृह्णीयात्।
    3. अवस्थात्रये मम पालनं कुर्यात्।
    4. धनादिगोपने मम सम्मतिं गृह्णीयात्।
    5. गवादि पशुक्रयविक्रये मम सम्मतिं गृह्णीयात्।
    6. वसन्तादि षट्सुऋतुषु मम पालनं कुर्यात्।
    7. सखी सुगन हास्यं कटुवाक्यम् न वदेत् न कुर्यात्। तदाहं भवतां वामांगे आगच्छामि।

(अथ द्वितीय सप्तपदी)

आदौ धर्मधरा कुटुम्बसुखदा मिष्टाप्रियाभाषिणी।
क्रोधालस्यनिवारिका सुखकरा आज्ञानुगावर्तिनी॥
शास्त्रानन्वयवृद्धशासनपरा धर्मानुगा सादरम्।
एते सौम्यगुणा वसन्ति सततं वामेहि सा त्वं भव॥

2. Google.com
3. Wikipedia.com
4. Yahoo.com

2A

Marriages of Strange Kinds (Across the World)

2A

MARRIAGES OF STRANGE KINDS (ACROSS THE WORLD)

This world so multi-farious, so vivid, so colourful, has some strange kinds of weddings which appear amusing and interesting also.

WEDDING UNDER WATER

This kind of marriages have recently been solemnized at Manila on 'Valentine Day' where in the bride and groom with a diving mask go in a deep aquarium and take the wedding vow.

GHOST MARRIAGE

It would startle to many a one that in some countries of world 'Ghost Marriages' are still prevalent as a relic of ancient civilization and China is one of such countries, where, in some provinces people arrange marriage for their dead son with all festivities & ceremonies of wedding having been performed there with. Ghost marriage is the result of the belief of people particularly in rural areas of China that even after death, their son remains in the form of ghost and would necessitate entertainment & joy with a female partner and the marriage with the dead woman is the answer. People in such areas purchase the dead body of a woman at a good price after matching the skeleton with their dead son & then go for all rituals of wedding. In spite of the crackdown by the Communist regime, Ghost marriages still exist in rural areas of some provinces of China.

TEMPORARY MARRIAGE FOR FEW HOURS

This kind of marriages is being hotly discussed in some Muslim Countries e.g. Iran etc to control and regulate illicit sexual relations. Such Marriages may have duration of one hour to 99 years, solemnized through 'Nikha Ceremony' and can be dissolved after few hours or so. However this has evoked a controversy being termed as anti-Islamic.

PRE-HISTORIC MARRIAGES

As transpires from the story mentioned in Mahabharata - the great epic, there existed a region with "Marriage Free" situation, where man and woman were free to choose and leave their partner as and when they desire without any rituals. Mahabharata perhaps describes the kind of marriages followed in Pre – Historic period as otherwise the institution of marriage was well established during Vedic period and the period of Mahabharata came there after.

GAY MARRIAGES

The Ist Gay Marriage of Delhi held between two girls Bubli and Gita. Now they are husband and wife.

Gay marriages are no longer of strange kind but are getting more and more popular in west and other countries across the world. A Gay marriage is a 'same sex' marriage, between man and a man, woman & a woman or between girl and a girl. Any one of the partners acts as husband and the other as wife with mutual consent. Many a countries of the world have recognized Gay marriages under 'Civil Partnership Act'. In India such marriages are not permissible as yet. However a first Gay marriage between two girls held recently in Delhi, has changed the course of history and may open the door for others.

3

The Institution of Marriage Evolution & Origin

3

THE INSTITUTION OF MARRIAGE
Evolution & Origin

The fun and frill, the grand show associated with marriages as of today, are not one day development but have taken millions of years to come in.

The first man and woman created by the almighty God must have taken years to learn the art of sex and thereafter procreation. In the beginning of the civilization the human beings were just gatherers of food and hunters. They would live in-groups and would lead a nomadic life. They moved from place to place in search of food and shelters. Man, woman and child lived in-groups to protect themselves from ferocious animals. As such, obviously there must have been utter laxity in the matter of sex. A possibility of marriage

In early days of civilization man was a hunter and food gatherer

Nicobar Islands where sexual laxity still exists among some tribes

less society has been mentioned in 'Mahabhata', wide obserwations made by Pandava brother Sahdev that in the land of Uttarkurush there was marriageless society in the city of Maheshmati. As and when civilisation developed and concept of families grew with members of a tribe got divided into families, living in the primary hutments which constituted a village. The institution of marriage must have set forth intially in a vague manner and then grew strong and stronger and well established to avoid chaoetic situation in the society.

HINDU PURANIC VERSION

Puranic version of Hinduism contains a good deal-what is fanciful as well as insteresting. Lord Brahma who is supposed to be creator of the world (Sarshti) using his Brahma power created some males - Sanat, Sanat Kumar, Sanandana etc. asking them to procreate Devour of any charm, attraction or interest in procreation, they left and engaged themselves in meditiation and became ascetic. Feeling dejected. Lord Brahma hit upon the idea of sexual activity that could attract individuals automatically by virtue of the enjoyment it was to involve. But it needed a different kind of creature meant to have sex with. So, the Lord created a man and a woman who were destined to set forth the process of sexual procreation. This first couple of a man and a woman was named 'Manu' and 'Shataroopa' who are believed to be the primordial ancestors of humankind. That is why each descendant of Manu came to be called as 'maanava'.

Lord Brahma - the creator of universe as per Hindu Mythology

Being irresistible, sexual activity could lead to a free-for-all situation to occur and created perfect chaoes in society. In order to avoid this situation, the leaders of the society decided to regulate and sanctify the process of matrimony relating it to certain rites i.e. social as well as religious. These rites included those carried out at the bridegroom's place before proceeding to the bride's place and those carried out at the bride's home before the arrival of the bridegroom. Besides, a number of rituals were linked to the solemnization of vivaaha-means to be carried away of the bride and the bridegroom together, now called a 'marriage'.

As matrimony involved a huge responsibility for either of the partners, the bridegroom and the bride, the rites related to it were shaped in such a way as to be full of enjoyment. music, dance, songs, decoration and the adornment of the couple in various ways came into vogue. Rich feasts, receptions and merry-making, extending over several days before and after the marriage ceremony also became a part and parcel of the matrimonial activity.

After the institution of marriage having had been created, to regulate and channelise the sexual activities and also procreation, a neccesity was felt to lend it an everlasting and permannet shape to establish appropraite social order. This calls for definite commitment and adherance to certain code of conduct on the part of both of the spouses and this was achieved by preseribing certain vows to be taken at the time of marriage linking it through a ritual of worship, the mode being different for each faith.

In case of Hinduism, Yajans played a dominating role in the development of civilization in ancient vedic period, so

Rituals in different faiths to sanctify a marriage

much so that offerings to Holy fire in the form of 'hawanas' were done twice a day, morning and evening. The vows were taken by husband and wife with fire God as witness and also invoking other Gods, making both the spouses accountable to the creator of the universe for fulfilment and adherance to these proclaimation - the ritual being called 'Satpadi' or 'Sat Phere', the chief ceremony of any Hindu marriage.

In case of Sikh marriage the ritual is called 'Laavan Reading' and in Bengali Marriage termed as 'Saat Pak'. Buddhist call this ritual as 'Vandna' and so on, so forth.

4

Modern Vs Ancient Concept of Marriage

4

MODERN Vs ANCIENT CONCEPT OF MARRIAGE

In many a western countries of the world and also in metro cities of India, marriage is fast becoming a means of fun and thrill. Procreation is taking a secondary place and rather back seat. The increasing trend of 'Gay Marriages' in many countries of the world is fast infecting India also. In such marriages the element of procreation is entirely missing. Several western countries have legalized 'Gay marriages' i.e. marriage with the person of the same sex. Reports appearing in new papers prove the point beyond doubt as under :

1. **Denmark** was the first country to recognize 'Gay marriage' as registered partnerships but different from a legal marriage, followed by **France** recognizing it a union between any two adults - man or woman - as a part of Civil Solidarity. **US**, Massachusetts, Vermont and Connecticut also recognize same-sex civil unions, while Hawaii, Maine, New Jersey and California allow couples living together, the same right as married couples.

2. **Netherlands** legalized gay marriages in April 2001. **Belgium** enacted Gay marriage in January 2003. **Canada** followed in June 2003. **Spain** allowed homosexual marriages from July 2003. **South Africa's** constitutional Court ruled in favour of same-sex marriages.

Even **U.K.** - the hub of western civilization, has also recently passed the act 'Civil Partnership Act' enabling the thousands of couple to marry with same sex.

Though in India homosexuality is banned and may lead to imprisonment but it may be difficult to stem the tide in view of the fact that more and more countries of the world are falling in league of Gay marriages. Such marriages are unnatural and do not have any sanctity from Indian point of view.

ANCIENT CONCEPT OF MARRIAGE :

In ancient India, a marriage has been regarded as a sacred religious ritual to enable a man, by becoming a householder, to perform sacrifices to the Gods to fulfill spiritual obligation and to procreate sons. Apasthamba Dharma Sutra indicates

that the main purposes of marriage are two viz. the wife enables a man to perform religious rites (ii) to procreate a son or sons who were supposed to save a man from hell. Also by taking seven steps together around the altar under 'Satpadi' ritual performed to solmnize and taking oath in presence of holy and divine fire God, the bride and groom are bound to associate with each other in fair & foul weather 'ups and downs' of life and above all in discharge of religious, social duties and obligations and are answerable to the creator of universe in case of default in any respect. A Rig Veda hymn[1] (X.85) blesses a bride : 'May you stay here together, may you not be separated, may you compass all life (long life), happy in your own house and playing with your sons and grandsons'.

According to Hindu Scriptures a person who is unmarried, is unholy[2] and religious sacrament performed by him would remain incomplete. Ramayana mentions that after the exile of Sita to forest when lord Rama performed Ashwamedha Yagya at Ayodhaya, the same problem arose and the strong opinion of the religious pundits was that the yagya being performed would not be fruitful till Sita and Rama would sit together to offer sacrifices to gods and to obviate this problem, the image of Sita was put with lord Rama to indicate her symbolic presence at the time of sacrament as she was on exile in forest in Valmiki Ashrama during the period of yajna. Even today a betel nut is kept by the side of a man in the absence of his wife.

Epic mentions a story of Subaru - the daughter of sage Kuni[3] who remained unmarried in all her life practicing severe penance. At the time of her death she found herself ineligible to go to heaven because her body was not consecrated by the sacrament of marriage.

WAS MARRIAGE ESSENTIAL FOR SALVATION?

The afore said Instance quoted from 'Mahabarata', one gains the impression that a person must get married for going to heaven after death. If we peep through the pages of vedic Indian history it will be found that the marriage though was considered most-desirable but was not regarded as absolutely necessary. The vedic literature mentions names of several Rishikas who made spiritual lineage and most of them were not married. However, in post vedic period and the period there after, the situation under went a change as many a 'Dharmsutras' as well as the message of 'Mahabarta', the marriage was deemed obligatory for a girl. The spell of Buddhism further strengthened the belief of people on account of the fact that many unmarried girls joined nunneries and they found wanting in their moral conduct later on and marriage was considered as the pre-emptive exercise in this regard.

A Nunnery of Buddism

This is, however, debatable as to why the high boundation of marriage was made applicable to women but not to men? For answer to this point one has to look back on the social circumstances prevailing in ancient period. There was no career avenues for women, even the opportunities of taking education were very scarce. There was no school or college like today, but one had to go far to a Guru at his hermitage for education under Strict regulations of discipline, conduct and above all to remain Bramchari for stipulated period upto the age of 16 to 25 years and obviously the parents would not send their daughter for education at a hermitage away from the haunt of city. Having been deprived of education opportunity, the women were unable to make advancement in any field e.g., literary, spiritual, performing arts etc. They would hang around parents, if they were alive and would be treated as burden by their brother in the event of their parents getting old, thus making their life more pitiable. As such making marriage obligatory, was prudent and necessary under the conditions mentioned above.

IS MARRIAGE, ONLY FOR PROCREATION?

From the above it need not infer that the ancient concept regards marriage as a means of procreation but not fulfillment of sexual urge. Infact, it will be a wrong interpretation of our scriptures which allow 'sex' observing certain constraints and injuncions at the occasion of religious functions or observing religious fast or at pilgrimage or in public places where such activities tentamount to misdemeanour or even sin. Lord Krishna in Bhagwat Gita clarifies that sex conforming[4] to tenets of Dharma as per scriptures and Shastras is my divinity (vibhuti).

Lord Triputi Shrine - pilgrimage

REFERENCES

1. Rig Veda X. 85
2. T. Br. II 2.2.6
3. Mahabharat IX.33
4. बलं बलवतां चाहं कामरागविवर्जितम्।
   धर्माविरुद्धो भूतेषु कामोऽस्मि भरतर्षभ।।

   - Srimad Bhagwad Gita 7.11

5

Marriages in Ancient India Kinds & Options

5

MARRIAGES IN ANCIENT INDIA KINDS & OPTIONS

The physical and geographical entity known as India, lying between the high Himalayas in the north and Cape Comorin (Kanya Kumari) in the south, and the two seas on the east and the west the frontier of which extended till Afghanistan during Maurya regime lived millions of human beings who would speak, apart from the innumerable dialects, at least twelve well known languages, each of which has its own literary style and literature, whose mode of dress, life and food differ considerably from each other, must be having many a forms of marriages. Also backward tribes of many states

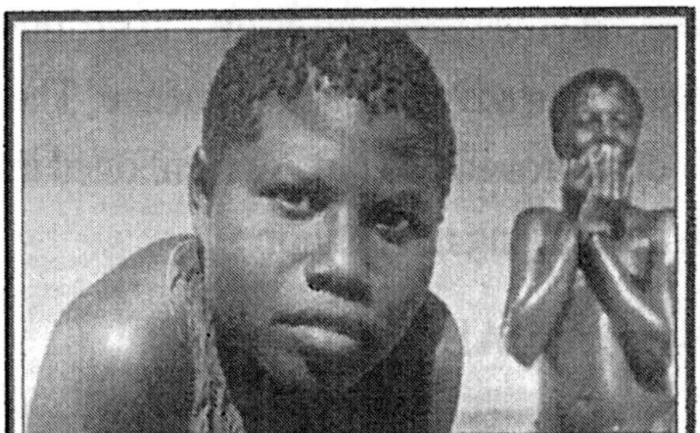

Some tribes in Nicobar Islands in primitive stage of civilization having sexual lexity.

have their own customs and manners entirely different from the regions there must have been many a ways of marriage. Also tribes still in primitive stage of civilization e.g. in Nicobar Island, there must still have some sexual laxity. Smrities and Dharma- Sutras, containing the regulations of marriage vary considerably from one another. No smriti of an age covers the entire india, but only a region, as such it is neigh possible to state all forms of marriage followed in ancient India or medieval India. However smrities have recognized the following forms of marriages (see Asvalayana Grhyasutra, (I.5.I-8; 6.1-8):

* Brahma Marriage
* Prajapatya Marriage
* Daiva Marriage
* Arsha Marriage
* Asura Marriage
* Gandharva Marriage
* Rakshasa Marriage
* Paisacha Marriage

Out of the above forms only the first four are approved as in these marriages, the groom is selected with due care taking into consideration the vital interest of bride, Gods are invoked for blessing the couple, holy fire is ignited in the form of yajna and to witness the vows taken by bride and groom to remain close companion in adversity and affluence. The remaining forms are not approved one but are mentioned in explicit manner, there by implying recognition.

BRAHMA MARRIAGE

This is the holiest form of marriage and is still being followed largely by the people, in diluted and amended form. Here the

bride is offered as gift – 'Dann' after decking her with valuable garments and jewels, to the bride groom, in the presence of parents or the head of family on either side. The consent of the bride and groom is implied. In ancient India when there was no telecommunication and no means of transport, the bride and groom living in different villages several miles away from each other, it was not possible to meet the bride and groom or to interact with each other before marriage. The search for groom was made through social contacts and selection was done by the father through his emissary keeping in view the social and financial status of the two families and compatibility. The marriage was then fixed on auspicious day to be performed in accordance with the procedure laid down in scriptures.

Sri Rama and his three brothers along with their respective consort performing 'Satpadi' ceremony in accordance with the system of Brahma form of Marriage

In today's India Brahma form of marriage is quite in vogue with the modification that selection of groom is made by the family of bride but the ultimate choice is left to the bride and groom before finalizing marriage. Of course the financial and social status of the family is also kept in view.

PRAJAPATYA MARRIAGE

The gift of a daughter, after the father has addressed the couple with the words "May both of you perform your religious duties together" and after he has honoured the groom (with Madhuparka, etc.), is declared to constitute the *Prajapatya form* of marriage.

Infact there is very little difference between *Brahma marriage* and that *Prajapatya form*. Both are almost identical.

In Prajapatya form also the marriage is solemnized after invoking Gods worshipping them, as per laid down procedure, i.e. igniting holy fire, tying knot, taking satpadi and exchanging vows for total commitment to each other, and active companionship etc. The only difference is that in Prajapatya form, the father of the bride addresses the couple for performing religious duties together through all the stages of life, thus emphaisizing the ever lasting companionship.

A question arises, what was the necessity to emphasize this point when the vows taken by the groom already cover this aspect and the possible interpolation may be that the four 'Ashrama System' spelling out four stages of life i.e. Brahmachari, house holder, Vanprasth and Sanyas, had been prevailing in ancient India, the father of the bride wished the cmpanionship of husband and wife through these stages.

The difference between Brahma and Prajapatya form of marriage being very little, smrities have deleted the Prajapatya form altogether.

DAIVA FORM OF MARRIAGE

When the father gives away his daughter after decking her with valuable garments and jewels to a Vedic scholar or priest, whom the father of the girl himself invites, it constitutes Diava Marriage.

On the face, it looks strange that a priest mostly Brahmin who is called upon to conduct the ritual of fire sacrifice i.e.

-Yajna is departed with the daughter of householder as it dilutes the holiness of the entire ritual defeating the very purpose for which Yajna was performed.

Many explanations are given in this regard. However, it is a fact that in ancient India towards the end of vedic period, the Yajnas formed a dominant role in day-to-day life of people. Broadly, Yajnas were divided into two categories, one called as *Nitya* which were to be performed daily by a householder and the other kind of yajnas were called as *Kamya* which were conducted to fulfill a particular wish of a person.

Even in small-small matters peoples would perform a Yajna expecting a desire-wish to be materialized. The same priest would be called upon every time and a familiarity developed between the householder and the priest resulting into marriage with priest after some period. However no satisfactory explanation is available in this regard.

ARSHA FORM OF MARRIAGE

Here the father of the girl chooses the groom and the daughter is given as gift, after taking one pair of cattle (a cow and a bull) or two pairs, only as a matter of fulfilling the law (and not as a sale of the girl), and this is named *Arsha Form.*

This form of marriage is still in vogue in many parts of India. The gift of one pair of cattle i.e. a cow & bull, is only symbolic and not a piece of price of bride as viewed by some of the Smriti writers. In fact the material value of one cow and one bull is insignificant against the fabulous gifts given by the parents of the bride comprising jewelry, valuable garments not only for the bride but for the family members also. Accepting huge gifts from the bride side & giving nothing looks rather odd and not keeping with the dignity of groom family. Even today some garments are given as gift from the groom side for the brothers of the bride.

ASURA MARRIAGE

When the girl is given away at the father's will after the bride-groom gives as much wealth as he can afford to pay to the relatives of the girl and to the girl herself, that is called the Asura form.

The Asura kind of marriage perhaps started under the justification that the father of the bride will lose one of his family members depriving him of useful service by way of marriage and would incur quite some expenditure in the marriage, as such he deserves due compensation for the same. This may be an excuse advanced by a greedy person for selling his daughter. The study of ancient literature shows that Asura Marriages were prevalent in ancient India. Mahabartha mentions, few would believe, that Gandhari was married to Dhritrashtra and Madri married to Pandva, following 'Asura System' of wedding and payments were made to the guardian of Gandhari as well as Madri by Bhishma in this behalf. Even Kakai was married to Dashrata in the similar manner.

From the above it need not infer that selling of bride under Asura System is permitted by Hindu culture. On the other hand it has been condemned in strong terms in different ages. Some of the preceptors have gone to the extent that they contempt the guardian of the bride with the warning that the selling of daughter will result into most terrible hell. Baudhayna Dharmsutra 11,201 refers. Similarly the Puranas also decry that the face of a man settling marriage for money is not worth seeing. Sometimes resort to Ex-communication of the person selling his daughter through marriage was also resorted to.

It may not be pertinent to mention that these historical marriages were not settled only for consideration of money as bride price, the royal status of the groom family must also have been prompted the guardian of bride agreeing for marriage.

GANDHARVA MARRIAGE

The union of a girl and the bride-groom by their mutual consent is known as Gandharva marriage which springs from the passion of love and has intercourse as its purpose.

Modern youths are getting more and more attracted towards this form of marriage where the mutual love is the only basis to form the union. In western countries almost all marriages in cities held now a days belonged, to this category. Even the people have gone one step further that they have already started to live as husband and wife and marriage is solemnized thereafter. The recent case of marriage held between the top film actors of Hollywood who were already living like husband and wife and even had a son was born through this union, the marriage was solemnized in most spactacular manner and was one of the most expensive matrimonail exercise incurring an expenditure of hundred crores of Rs in Indian currency. As regards ancient India, there is a controversy whether this type of marriage should be treated as approved form of marriage, some of the preceptors regard it as an approved marriage while the others disapprove vehemently. The main objection being that in such marriages the rituals are not performed and the couple has already consummated their marriage after falling in love. In India improvised version of

Gandharva form of marriage is picking up by removing the scriptural objection of not performing ritual before the marriage and accordingly after the couple has fallen in love both spouses inform their parents of their love affairs, who many a times in their wisdom, had to agree for the marriage which is solemnized as Brahma marriage.

GANDHARVA MARRIAGE- MODERN STYLE

Imagine A Scene

'A big pandal pitched on the road side park, decked up with guests, entrance gate decorated beautifully, flower pots, hanging garlands, and stylish fountain, lavish carpets and sofa, chairs well arranged inside and a stage- dias specially prepared with two matrimonial chairs placed upon it for 'Varmala ceremony' of the marriage to be celebrated on it. The marriage party few yards away from the shiamyana with band, music, decorating lights, fire works and groom arode on a beautiful horse proceeding toward the venue of marriage'.

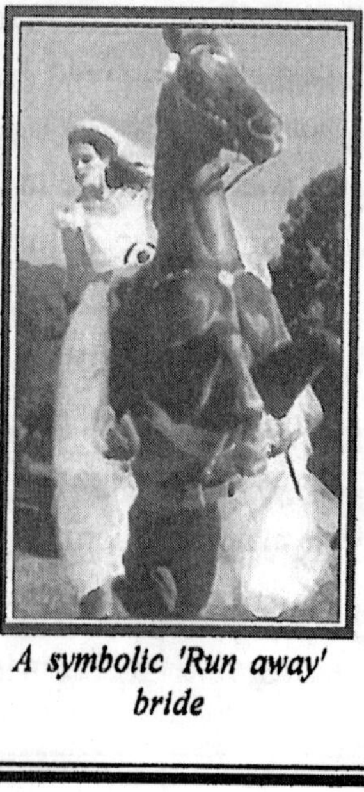

A symbolic 'Run away' bride

Suddenly a speeding car stops near the pandal gate. The bride in her wedding dress and jewellry gets down the car but instead of going inside the pandal crosses over the road to reach another car already waiting for her and she immediately gets in the car and runs away with another person (possibility her lover) sitting there in. The marriage party enters the pandal and the groom proceeds to the 'Varmala stage' prepared for the ceremony. But there is no trace of bride. The parents, the relatives all are badly perplexed and fail to find the bride anywhere. A word spreads among the participants regarding the missing bride with worried relatives running here and there.

Such cases of elopement of bride are on increasing side in metro cities now a days and speak the modern style of Gandharva Marriage.

RAKSHASA FORM OF MARRIAGE

Bhishma forcibly carrying away the three daughters of King of Kasi.

In Rakshasa form of marriage, force is used to carry away the bride and to marry her thereafter. In today's language it is a case of pure kidnapping and raping and is severely punishable under the Act of law.

However, if we see through the prism of vedic India, Aryans had to fight several battles with non-Aryans. A hymn of Rigveda mentions "Oh Indra! Destroyer of foes, kill them. Destroy the Dasa race. We are surrounded on all sides by Dasya tribe'. This warrior like mentality i.e. to wrest away any thing through the power of his arms, resulted into Rakshasa form of marriage. In Brahma Kind of marriage the bride is given as a gift or charity (Kanyadaan) and the dignity of kshtriya does not allow to accept a charity when he has the power of arms to get the same. However, the bride's consent in this regard is completely ignored. The girl not willing for getting married to a person who has got her as booty of war, has to yield for marriage and no other option is left for her, thus doing gross injustice to a human being.

Some of the scholars treat the marriage between Subhadra and Arjuna as well as Rukmini with Shri Krishna as Rakshasa marriage in Mahabharta period, ignoring the important point that Subhadra had already fallen in love with Arjuna; and she was about to marry the son of Dhristhrastra unwillingly. Similarly Rukmini had sent even love letters to Shri Krishna expressing her sincere desire for marriage with him. As such these marriage are correctly termed as Gandharva-cum-Rakshasa marriages.

Arjuna carries away Subhadra in a chariot

The clear instance of Rakshasa marriage is available in Mahabharta when Bhishma after defeating the king of Kasi carried away his daughters- Amba, Ambika and Ambalika against the wish of those girls and this is purely the Rakshasa marriage and was criticized by the other kings. In modern India such marriage has no place in society and is treated a heinous crime.

PAISACHA MARRIAGE

In the language of today this is not a marriage but a rape of wicked kind and may land a person in a jail and even life term imprisonment. In this kind of marriage a person makes the bride to yield to his passion forcibly and over powering her or intoxicating her by over drinking or by magic through a tail man. It has been called *Paisacha Marriage* as a *Paisacha is a Goblin* known for this kind of sinister act. This is the most condemnable and sinful form of all kinds of marriages.

Why this has been called a marriage at all, can be interpolated in simple manner. In conservative society of ancient India, virginity carried a high premium for marriage and a girl whose virginity has been violated and the same comes to light, would not be acceptable by a respectable person for the purpose of marriage and this will mean adding a salt to her injury. On one hand she was the victim of rape and on the other, she was unacceptable by the society for all the time to come. Under these circumstances rehabilitation of the unfortunate girl was too difficult. The only way she could be helped was - by forcing the wrong doer to marry the girl subject to her consent. And the latter, many a times would agree to the arrangement, provided there is some compatibility in regard to age, look, and social status. Even today many a cases of rape are settled accordingly by the court of law.

SVAYAMVARA MARRIAGE

In simplest form, the *Svayamvara Marriage* occurs when a girl, who attains puberty and whose father does not find a proper husband, herself seeks, her husband. Yajnavalkya I.64 also recommends 'Svayamvara' to every girl when there is no parent or other guardian who could find a worthy husband for her daughter. *Svayamvara form* of marriage is a kind of Gandharva marriage and was in vogue during Gupta Age also.

This finds mention in the works of *Kalidasa*- a famous Dramatist and poet of the period.

Svayamvara Marriage has two varieties. The one where the passion of love is the bedrock of the marriage. In the other kind which finds mention in Epic period, the selection of groom is made by testing his valour or skill in Dhanurveda. Invitations are sent to kings and others for Svayamvara ceremony and are given a test and whosoever emerges winner in the test is chosen as the groom and is garlanded by the bride on the spot, regardless of age, caste, creed or family antecedents. The wedding of Sita with Rama, and Draupadi with Pandvas were held as Svayamvara Marriage.

Svayamvara Marriage Ceremony of Sita

REFERENCE AND BIBLOGRAPHY

1. *Asvalayana Grhyasutra* - I.5.I-8; 6.1-8

2. *Mahabharata*, Gita Press Gorakhpur.

3. *Manu Smriti,* Chaukhmbha Prakashan, Vanarasi

4. *Yajnalka Smriti*, Chaukhambha Prakashan, Vanarasi

5. *Bandhyana Dharm Sutra*, C.P. Benaras

6. *Srimad Bhagwat Purana*, Gita Press, Gorakhpur

7. *Ram Chrit Mansa* by Goswami Tulsi Das.

6

Ceremonies of Marriage in Ancient India

6

CEREMONIES OF MARRIAGE IN ANCIENT INDIA

- Vedic Period
- Post Vedic Period
- Gupta Age
- Medieaval India

The institution of marriage in ancient India was not only well established but wedding was considered a memorable event celebrated in pompous manner with grandeur and gaiety.

Ancient Indian text employs different words to denote the event of marriage. The word 'Vivaha' occurs in the Taittiriya

Samhita (VII.2.87) & Aitareya Brahmana (27.5). This means taking the girl away in special way or for a special purpose i.e. making her one's wife. Other word 'Udvaha Prenaya' also carries similar meaning. There is a recent trend to use the word 'Panigrahan-means taking the hand of the girl. (This is done at the time of Saptpadi (Saat Phere).

THE VEDIC PERIOD:

Vedic Period is the most ancient period marking the dawn and meridian of Aryan civilization when the Aryans mostly got settled in small villages some of which developed into towns later on.

The Preffix ॐ with prayer hyms of Rigveda

Vedas which are considered sacred literature of Hinduism and are the oldest literary work (especially the Rigveda) have a very important place in the history of world civilization. The hymns of Vedas are still looked upon as revealed words of God. In fact the entire culture and religion of Hindu civilization have been evolved on the bed rock of these Vedas.

THE RIG VEDA:

Out of the four Vedas, Rig Veda is considered as the most ancient of all scriptures and gives an idea of the sublime doctrine and fountain of Aryan civilization. As regards the marriage ceremonies held in the age of Rig-Veda; the hymn in Rig Veda (X.85) gives us some idea of the marriage ritual.

THE OLDEST CEREMONY OF MARRIAGE

The hymn RV (x.85) narrates the marriage of Soma and Surya (the daughter of the Sun). The marriage of Surya with Soma is narrated in verse 6-16. Surya is the ideal charming maiden going to be married with an ideal young man - Soma. The Sun celebrates the marriage of his daughter and the whole world is invited to assemble (X. 17.1). The bridegroom and party proceed to the bride's house (X.17.1), where the well-adorned bride remains ready (IV.58.9) to join the marriage-feast. The ceremony proper now commences. The bridegroom grasps the hand of the bride and leads her round the fire (X.85.36,38). These two acts constitute the essence of the marriage and the bridegroom is now the husband who takes her by his hand (Hasta-graabha : X.18.8). The bridegroom next takes the bride home in a chariot, in procession (X. 85.7, 8, 10, 24-27, 42). Then follows the consummation which is signified chiefly by the purification of the bride's garment (X.85. 28-30, 35). A special garment was worn by the bride at the marriage ceremony; and was called *vadhuya.* Another verse (R.V.X. 18.8) exhorts a widow to remarry and live happily.

AGE OF YAJUR VEDA AND SAMAYEDA

In this period yajnas i.e. fire offering played an important part of day to day life. The people would perform yajna daily even twice morning and evening for which altars were constructed in different shapes and this holds good for altars to solemnize the marriage which otherwise remained similar as in Rigveda period. However there was one important addition to the ceremony that the bride was got to mount a stone before grasping her hand.

ATHARVA VEDA

The elements of the marriage ceremony described in the marriage hymns of the Rig Veda are reproduced without much change in the corresponding Atharvaveda-hymns, with the same important feature, which later became essential, namely the bridegroom causing the bride to mount a stone before grasping her hand.

Yajurveda gives a detailed description of the qualities of brides and bridegrooms. A brahmachari, who becomes the husband is an intellect as well as the master of different sciences. He is the embodiment of gentlemanliness and the lord of wealth. He is the abode of all virtues (Y.V. VIII. 1-30; XI. 39, 50-55, 57). Yajurveda also says that a person should take in wedlock the girl, who like the pure water is full of vast intellect and learning, good looking and well-behaved, full of glory to please her husband in his beautiful home; and make him happy and contented. The couple should respect each other (Y.V. XII. 35)[1].

MARRIAGE PROCESSION

One hymn in the Atharvaveda clearly mentions the bridal procession comparing bride's spirit as bridal car, the canopy thereof as heaven, both husband and wife as the drivers of the chariot of the domestic life (A.V. XIV. I. 10-11). Music, both vocal and instrumental, and dancing continue to be among the amusements of this age. Several professional musicians are known, and the variety of instrumental music in vogue can be inferred from the types of musicians enumerated, such as lute-players, flute-players, conch-blowers, drummers, etc. Among the musical instruments known are the aghati (cymbal) to accompany dancing, drums, flutes, and lutes of various types, and the harp or lyre with a hundred strings. These instruments might have been played during the marriage procession.

During the Vedic period the wife lived in the husband's house. One hymn in the Rg Veda mentions the bridal journey as " O bride, ascend the chariot, made of good kimsuka wood and of salmali. It is multiform, decorated with gold, well-covered, well-wheeled. May your world of married life have the happiness of the immortals"(RV. X.85.20) Atharvaveda says "I set her free from her parental home, but not from that of her husband ....Go to the house of your husband to be the household's mistress ...." (A.V. XIV. 1. 18-20).

A chariot for bride

THE POST-VEDIC PERIOD

The post Vedic period spanning 800B.C. to the beginning of Christian era is marked by a glaxy of eminent preceptors like Yagya valkya, Panini, Manu, Gautam, etc. who through their works titled as Dharamasutra and Smiriti, stipulated detailed regulations on various matters of day-to day life e.g. education, birth celebration, and marriage for which elaborate procedure was prescribed for various rituals. Performing puja of various dieties at the time of marriage, the wedding vows,

Kanaya-Daan, treating marriage as a Daan of bride etc. Ganesh puja was considered mandatory for marriage and pre marriage rituals to wardoff obstacles and difficulties in performance of marriage. Consideration of Gotra of the father and mother of bride as well as groom and also the close relationship with them was felt necessary while fixing the marriage.

The science of astronomy which grew during Rig Vedic period, developed further and was made use of, determining the auspicious date and time of marriage. The kundli of bride and groom as well as matching manglik dosha were also taken

Astrology in Marriage fixations

into consideration for marriage, which was treated as a sanskar named as 'panigrahn sanskar'. The concept of solar system also came in, with 9 Planets, treating Sun as stationary and Earth revolving around the Sun. Worship of these 9 Planets called 'Nav Graha' was also introduced for peace and calm in regard to performance of ritual.

WHAT VARIOUS GRIH SUTRAS SAY

Asvalayana-grhya-sutra deals with all the marriage rites as follows: Having placed to the west of the fire (that is kindled on the altar) a mill-stone and to the north-east (of the fire) a water jar, he (groom) should offer sacrifice (with sruva), while the bride takes hold of him (touches his right hand) standing with his face turned to the west, while the bride is sitting and has her face turned to the east. He should seize only her thumb with the mantra 'I take hold of thy hand for happiness', if he desires that only male children be born to him. However he may seize her other fingers if he is desirous of female children; he may seize her hand on the hair side together with the thumb if he is desirous of both (male and female children). Leading her thrice round the fire and the water jar so that their right sides are turned towards (the fire) he murmurs: 'I am ama (this), thou art sa (she), thou art sa, I am ama; I am heaven, thou art the ..earth.... Let us both marry here.... Let us beget offspring.... Each time he leads her round (the fire), he makes her tread on the stone with certain words. Having first poured clarified butter over her joined hands, the bride's brother or some one who is in the place of brother pours fried grain twice over the bride's joined hands, three times in the case of those whose gotra is Jamadagni (i.e., if the bridegroom is of that gotra). Then he pours clarified butter over what has been cut off (separated from the aggregate). This is the rule about the portions to be cut off (in every case where there is avadana). Then the girl offers sacrifice to different Gods.

There are three parts in the samskara of marriage with certain rites that are preliminary, there are then a few rites that are of the essence of the samskara viz., panigrahana, homa, going round the fire and the saptapadi, and there are certain rites like - seeing of the Pole Star and etc. that are subsequent to the central rites. The essential rites are mentioned by all Sutrakaras, but as to the preceding and subsequent rites there is a great divergence in the details. As regards the essential rites the sequence in which they take place differs. For example, the *Asvalayan grhya sutra* (17.7) describes going round the fire before *saptapadi*, while the *Apastambagrhyasutra* describes *saptapadi* (IV. 16) before the act of going round the fire (V.1). The *Gobhila grhya* (II.2.16), the *Khadira grhyasutra* (I.3.31) and *Baudhayana grhyasutra* (I.4.10) describe panigrahana after *saptapadi* while many other *sutrakaras* describe it before *saptapadi* Among the principal ceremonies in marriage described by Kalidasa in the

Concept of nine planets (Navgrah)

Raghuvamsa VII are *madhuparka, homa,* going round the fire, panigrahana, *laja-homa* and *aardraakshataropana.*

In the *Gobhila Grhyasutra* it is said "Leading forward towards the sacred fire (from the house) the bride who is wrapped in a robe and wears the sacred thread (slung from her left shoulder in the Yajnopavita mode) he (the husband) should murmur the verse 'Soma gave her to Gaandharva'. The bride had to wear her garments (at the time of the wedding) in the form of yajnopavita. Manu says that the ceremony of marriage is the only samskara performed with Vedic mantras in the case of woman, attendance on the husband amounts to serving a guru (which a student had to do) and performance of domestic duties to worship the fire (which the student had to perform by offering a fuel-sticks in the morning and evening every day).

SELECTION OF A BRIDE AND BRIDEGROOM

Asvalavana gr. (1.5.2) says 'one should give a maiden[2] (in marriage) to a man endowed with intelligence'. Manu gives a detailed description of the qualities of the bride, bridegroom and their families (111.2-44). The Apasthamba grhyasutra (3.20) remarks the accomplishments of a bridegroom that he must be endowed with good family, a good character, auspicious characteristics, learning and good health. Asvalayan (1.5.1) and others place kula (a good family) in the forefront in the case of both the bride and the bridegroom.[3] Asvalayana gr. (1.5.3) says 'one should marry a girl who is endowed with intelligence, beauty, a good character and auspicious characteristics and who is healthy'.

The various stages of the marriage ceremony are as follows: (I) the wooer formally goes to the girl's house (2) when the bride's father has given his formal consent, the bridegroom performs a sacrifice; (3) early in the morning of the first day of the marriage celebrations the bride is bathed (4) a sacrifice is offered then by the high priest of the bride's family and a dance of four or eight women (not widows) takes place as part of the Indrani karman; (5) the bridegroom then goes to the girl's house and makes the gift of a garment, and mirror etc. to the bride who has been bathed as mentioned already; (6) The Kanya-pradana or the formal giving away of the bride now takes place, followed (7) by the Panigrahana - the clasping of the bride's right hand by the bridegroom with his own right hand; (8) the treading on stone (9) the leading of the bride round the fire by the bridegroom; (10) the sacrifice of fried grains; and, the most important ceremony of all (11) the saptapadi, the couple walking seven steps together as symbolic of their lifelong concord, follow in due order. Finally the bride is taken in to her new house.

FEAST

During the wedding, athiti or guests, were first offered madhuparka, i.e., a mixture of curds, honey, and ghi. After this, food containing sweet was to be offered.

During the Mauryan period it was normal to throw a feast on ceremonial or auspicious occasions like births and marriages. Anyone giving a large feast was asked to make special drainage arrangements for washing (3.8.8). The king himself, duly protected, attended such feasts[4] (1.21.28).

MARRIAGE PROCESSION

The Atharvaveda gives a glimpse of bridal car.[5] Dancing, and both vocal and instrumental music, were well cultivated right from the Vedic age. In the marriage ceremony the bridegroom sings a gatha after treading on the stone by the bride. The vogue of the musical recitations of the Samaveda is followed by way of a general expiation, at the end of every ceremony.

MARRIAGES DURING GUPTA AGE

Gupta Age from 4th to 8th century A.D. is the unique period in the Indian history and is called the golden period of ancient India. The use and deployment of elephants for various purposes which started during Nanda & Maurya period became more and more common. Even in marriages especially by royal and affluent families elephant well decorated

Elephant ride for groom

was deployed as a ride for groom as well as his family members.

As evinced from the works of the Kalidasa- who was a great poet and dramatist of Gupta period the system of marriages transpires as under :

After completing his studies at the age of sixteen or after finishing his travels and further studies at thirty, the brahmacharin was permitted to marry and enter the Grihastha asrama. Kalidasa attaches much importance to the samskara of marriage and according to him, no religious rite was to be performed by a man without wife. Even the everyday sacrifice was to be performed jointly with the wife.

Kalidasa refers to four kinds of marriages: Svayamvara, Prajapatva, Gandharva and Asura. Svayamvara was conducted in the court when several kings sought the hand of a princess. The princess either made the selection or accepted one who performed certain feats.

In the Prajapatya form of marriage, the father gave away his fully ornamented daughter to the bridegroom. This was probably the most popular. The ceremony was performed by the purohita before agni which was considered a witness. Ghritam (clarified butter) and other things were offered to the fire. After the ceremony, householders threw wet rice on the couple and the guests presented gifts to them.

The Gandharva type of marriage was contracted by lovers without consulting parents and without performing any ritual.

In the Asura type, the boy paid bride-money (duhitra-sulka) as a condition of marriage. This system still exists in many parts of India for example in Kashmir.

MARRIAGE DURING MEDIEVAL PERIOD

With the advent of Muslims in this country after the defeat of Prithiavi Raj Chauhan, the political as well as social scenario underwent a change. The Muslim culture also begun to make a dent on Hindu society. The veil system which is an important part of Muslim culture gripped the Hindu women also as commonly believed. The bride in her law's house would keep

Veil system in Muslim Culture

her face and forehead clad with saree or chuni in front of her elders like father-in-laws, uncle-in-laws, elder-brothers of her husband, etc. The age of marriage came down to as low as 8 years and the parents would start worrying if their daughter crosses the age of 9 and is not got married.

In medieval period few more rituals were added as mentioned in medieval Digests :

1. Simantapujana: Honouring the bridegroom and his party on their arrival at the bride's village.
2. Gauri-Hara puja. Worship of 'would be bride' as embodiment of Godess Gauri.
3. Taila-haridraropana: Applying turmeric powder to the bridegroom's body and bride's body. (Batna Ceremony)

4. Mangalasutra-bandhana: Tying a string having golden and other beads on it round the neck of the bride
5. Uttariyapranta-bandhana: Tying turmeric pieces and betelnut on to the end of the upper garments of both and making a knot of their two garments together.

A Palki ride for bride

REFERENCES :

1. आपो देवी: प्रति गृभ्णीत भस्मैतत्स्योने
   कृणुध्वᳬ सुरभा उ लोके।
   तस्मै नमन्तां जनय: सुपत्नीर्मातेव पुत्रं
   विभृतप्स्वेनत्।। - *YV.XII. 35*
2. बुद्धिमते कन्यां प्रयच्छेत। *As. G.S.1.5.2*
3. कुलमग्रे परीक्षते ये मातृत: पितृतश्चेति यथोक्तं पुरस्तात्।
4. बुद्धिरूपशीललक्षणसंपन्नामरोगामुपयच्छेत्
5. AV. XIV. I. 10-16 (Devi Chand M.A.)

7

Infidelity & Adultery in Ancient india

7

INFIDELITY & ADULTERY IN ANCIENT INDIA

The Institution of Marriage is founded on the bed rock of honesty, integrity, love and faith. It calls for trust and total commitment to go together to traverse the Mundane journey of life in happiness and sorrow, up & down, poverty riches and so on.

In a marriage of the kind we all yearn to have, fidelity is vital. It implies a commitment that's total and complete. You seek the closest intimacy possible from no one else, so sweet is the love you receive. What could be more reassuring and more meaningful? But a relationship that we all crave for, comes with a price tag and that is fidelity. None can repair that first fine careless rupture, once trust is ruptured it is ruptured forever. It is a betrayal that leaves you feeling painfully inadequate.

Infidelity in Ancient India was regarded as one of the serious misdemeanours by a woman and has been condemned in clear terms; so much so that seriptures say that such women would earn the curse of God and may get widow again and again in their next birth-after-birth. Even today infidelity is condemned by society though not regarded as crime but may result into *DIVORCE* under the law of the land.

According to Yajnavalkya (1.70, 72) 'an adulterous women should be deprived of her authority (over servants etc.), should be made to wear dirty cloths, should be given food just sufficient to enable her to live, should be treated with scorn and made to lie on the ground (not on a cot)'.

Manu IV. 133 for bids adultery with another's wife and observes that there is nothing that harms one's life as much as adultery. The Mitakshara points out that the wives of Brahminas, Kshtriyas, and Vaisyas who commit adultery with Sudra may be purified by a penance in case no child is born (of the intercourse), but not otherwise. According to Vasishta (Xxi. 10) only four types of wives are to be abandoned, viz, one who has intercourse with the husband's pupil and with the husband's guru, and especially one who attempts to kill her husband and who commits adultery with a man of degraded caste.

If one goes through various laws regarding adultery many of them propounded rather mild punishments. Veda Vyasa (II. *49-50)* says that 'a wife who is guilty of adultery should be kept in the house but devoid of her rights of associating in religious and conjugal matters and of her rights over property, and should be treated with scorn; but when she has had monthly course after the act of adultery, the husband should allow her the usual rights of wife as before.

Ramayana mentions a story of Ahilya speaking of strict fidelily, a women was expected to adhere to, during that period.

'Rishi Gautam' was living with his wife Ahilya in his ashram near the bank of a holy river; once went to take bath in the river informing his wife that he would return soon after taking bath and performing Pooja.

The Moon God seeing her alone and stung by her beauty, could not resist his sexual urge and approached her, disguising himself as Rishi Gautam and persuaded her to yield to his sexual passion. After all was over and the Moon God left for his abode, Rishi Gautam returned after taking bath as usual.

Utterly surprised Ahilya revealed her story to his husband who fumed in anger and treated it as an act into infidelity on the part of his wife, and hurled a curse on her to get jammed as a dead life less stone to be restored to her life when Shri Rama on his incarnation at Ayodhya would pass through the hermitage and would touch her with his feet. This speaks how seriously the infidelity was treated in ancient India.

Further the story of Parshuram who is regarded as incarnation of Lord Vishnu is another instance of strict fidelity expected from a woman.

Rishi Jamdagni, the father of Shri Parshuram asked his wife Renuka to bring holy water from river Ganges for performing Yajna. On reaching the bank of the river Ganges, Renuka saw Gandharv's King 'Chitrath' bathing with his queens with overtures of water romance . Renuka got so absorbed seeing the water romance that she forgot to return to her husband with holy water for Yajna. In fact the sight of water romance aroused a sexual feeling in her also. This delayed her to return to her husband with water who raged into anger and asked the reason of being abnormally late. Treating it as an instance of violation

of infidelity on the part of Renuka, Jamdagni asked his sons to kill their mother but all of them refused to comply with the order keeping in view that the killing of mother is highly a sinister act. At last Mahrishi Jamdagni called his youngest son 'Parshuram' and asked him to kill Renuka, the mother of parshuram. It was difficult task for Parshuram and he was between deep and devil. Neither he wanted to kill his mother nor to disobey his father. However keeping in mind the super powers attained by Rishi - Jamdagni through tapas he complied with the order of his father and killed his mother as well as brothers. This satisfied and pleased Rishi Jamdagni and he granted boon to Shri Parshuram for resloration his mother and brothers to life again.

Smirtis elaborately describe the rewards of wife's devotion to her husband. According to Manu (IX.29-30;V. 165 & 164) a woman who does not prove faithless to her husband in thought, word and deed secures the heavenly worlds together with her husband and is spoken of as a sadhvi (Pativrata), but by proving faithless to her husband, a woman incurs censure in this world, is born as a female jackal (in the next life) and is afflicted with very bad diseases. Yajnavalka (1.75 and 87) declares that woman, who does not approach another while the husband is living or after his death attains glory in this world and plays with Uma (the wife of Shiva) in heaven.

Anusasanaparva (146. 4-6) names several pativratas of ancient times. Ancient Indian literature eulogizes the great pativratas like Arundhati, Damayanti, Sandili, Savitri, Sita, Anasuya, Satya and others).

REFERENCES :

1. Manu Smriti - Chakhambha Prakashan, Vanarasi
2. Yajaualka Smriti - Chakhambha Prakashan, Vanarasi
3. Baudhyana Dharm Sutra
4. Ram Charit Mansa - Goswami Tulsi Dass
5. Srimad Bhagwad Purana, Gita Press, Gorakhpur

8

Romance
Ancient Vs Modern

8

ROMANCE

ANCIENT VS MODERN

We are living in a world, which is getting more and more romantic, more and more funny, thrilling. One can share moments of fun as a spectator in parks, jungles, water, air and everywhere. Hardly there is any newspaper or magazine not displaying romantic scene. Almost all the cinema films are dominant with various kissing postures and the new ways of romance. This art has taken fast strides in modern days.

Gone are the days when in Ancient India bushes, fields of crops on the out skirt of a village, isolated and abandoned broken houses with debris spread here and there, were the ideal sites for romance which was strictly a private affair and even a minor sight of a passer by would rattle the loving couple, and grasping of hand was considered a serious misdemeanour

on the part of the couple. With a great change transforming the thinking and minds of the people, grasping of hands no longer attracts the stare of the passers by. Romance has come in wide open and even in groups and mass gathering.

Old and New

In ancient age funny and fanciful methods and tricks were used to woo a beloved and to win her heart, black magic, tantrik vidhya, tail man and other such devices were employed. With no means of transport or communication, no other option was available.

The Atharva Veda is full of instances mentioning the youth and young maidens to use the magic and spells to win the heart of their counter part. (Hymns of Atharva Veda refer).

Lord Krishna in Sri Mad-Bhagvad Gita says that a person 'Yogi' having absorbed himself in deep meditation with controlled senses and perfect union of 'chita' (soul) with almighty God, attains superb happiness and pleasure which surpasses all kind of enjoyment. Whereas the modern erotic scholars say that the enjoyment which emanate from the sexual union of two human beings is superb and most enjoyable and one can attain the ultimate from this union Shri Mad Bhagvad Gita though admits the excellence of sexual enjoyment but denounces this form of enjoyment as being momentry and temporary.

The new age of informatics has ushered in a new era and has proved a boom to the loving couples, chatting through internet, post offices and courier services, news papers have come in a big way to convey the romance feeling and expression of love. Mobile phones have made things dam easy in ensuring total privacy to the over tures of love and romance. The 'Valentine Day' being celebrated as a day of romance is earning a wide popularity for expression of romance through presenting the bunch of roses.

Modern Romance starts from 'dating' or grasping of hands & goes more erotic & sexual gradually.

MODERN ROMANCE STEP BY STEP

I

II

III

IV

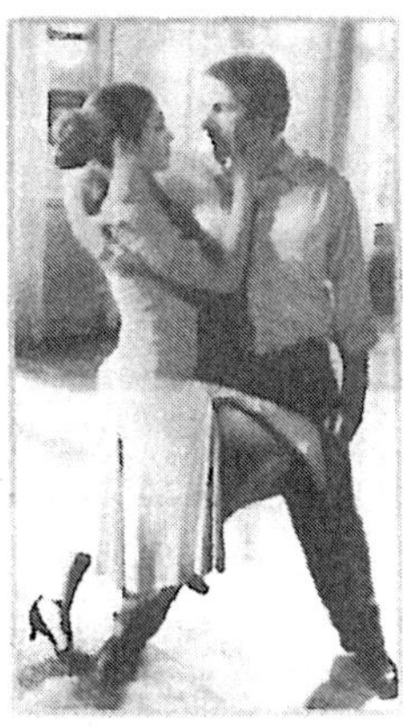

V

ROMANCE IN OPEN

Tango Dance Competition

ANCIENT INDIA

If we dare to peep into past centuries of India beginning from vedic period we will see that India was not only a country of sages, saints and snake charmers but has history of romance and there are many recorded cases of the effect in ancient scriptures.

WORLD'S FIRST KNOWN ROMANCE

Rig-Veda considered as the most ancient scripture on Earth mentions the story of King Puruavsa who fell in love with a nymph 'Urvashi' and married her with certain conditions. The romance continued for several years with all kinds of romantic manoeure i.e. embrace, lifting up in lap and other such overtures to the extent of mating her thrice in a day. The hymns of Rig-Veda are regarded as the holywords of God, enjoying unstinted faith of Hindus and are considered authentic as such Romance story reveals the sexual passion of ancients in a very candid manner.

ROMANCE OF VISHWAMITRA

Imagine a scene – "Bank of a holy river agog with sweet and sparkling water flowing therein with melodious sound, lush green grassy tract of land, grove formed of branches and leaves and the long staple of grass, a charming and romantic environment, a nymph with unparalleled beauty and silky velvet

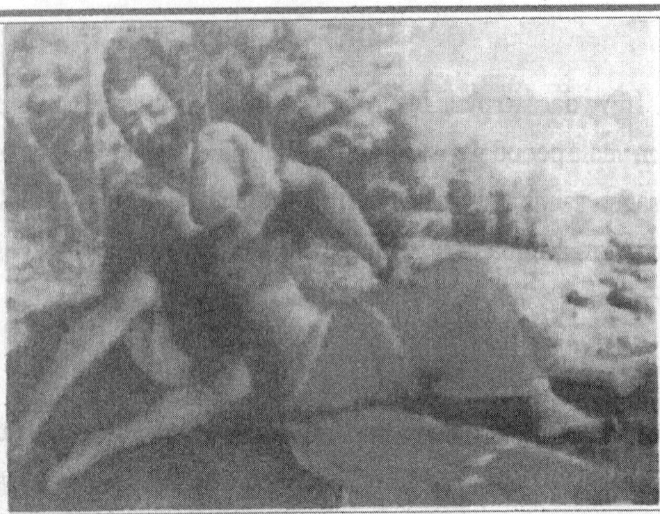

hair, catchy eyes, lying in the lap of a hermit in semi-exposed posture with her head supported by the arm of a sage and with no thought of time, and nobody is nearby to question, romance at high pitch" – this is the story of sage-Vishwamitra.

Vishwamitra, a Vedic Rishi who has given a unique Gayatri Mantra (Om Bhoo Bhuva Suvah...) still chanted all over India by all Hindus even today, when he was undergoing strict penance (Tapa) to acquire super natural powers, created a fear in the mind of Indra – the King of heaven that the ascetic sage wanted to acquire his empire of heaven, drafted a nymph - Menaka to seduce the sage - Vishwamitra to diminish his power. Menaka succeeded to allure the ascetic sage and their romance continued for quite some time resulting into the birth of a baby 'Shakuntala'.

SUBTLE AND IDEAL ROMANCE BY SHRI RAMA

Shri Rama who is worshiped as God by lakhs of Hindus, presents an example of ideal and subtle romance as mentioned in Ramayana. Accompanied with sage Vishwamitra, Shri Rama and Lakshman while going to participate in Swamvar ceremony organized by King Janaka for the marriage of his daughter Sita, made a brief halt in Janak Vatika, a decorated park on the out skirts of Janakpuri. Coincidentally Sita also visits the decorated park and pours her glance over Shri Rama and both see each other with romantic feeling. Shri Rama smiles a bit little moving his lips and Sita on seeing him for a minute, looks and chooses him as the best bet for marriage. This lasted only for few minutes making Sita to pray goddess Gauri to grant her wish of marriage with Shri Rama who divulges his heart feelings to Lakshman also. This constitutes a romance of most subtle kind.

SPRIRITUAL ROMANCE BY SHRI KRISHNA WITH GOPIKAS

Divine romance named as "Ras Leela" of Lord Krishna with Gopikas at Vrindavan and Gokul is well known to every Hindu. Srimad Bhagwad Purana mentions a diligence of Lord Krishna with 11,000 Gopis who came out of their houses. Shri Krishna plays on flute with sweet melodies.

They assemble in the shadow of Kadamb tree rallying around Shri Krishna enjoying with hide and seek, some time twisting and dancing with Shri Krishna and all other overtures. Radha, a married woman has closest intimacy with Shri Krishna. She even shares flute recital with Lord Krishna.

SRI MAD BHAGVAD PURANA DESCRIBES A SCENE OF A 'RAS PLAY' AS UNDER:

(Now)[1] commenced duly the festive dance of Rasa adorned with the circle of the aforesaid Gopis standing with their necks encircled by (the arms of) Sri Krsna the Master of Yoga (inconceivable powers), who (appeared to have) introduced Himself (in so many identical forms) between every two Gopis, and whom those (cowherd) women imagined to be by their own side. There in the company of those girls Lord Sri Krsna (the Son of Devaki) shone exceedingly bright like a large emerald strung in the midst of (every two) gold beads. With their (measured) treads, the motions of their hands, the playful movements of their eye-brows, accompanied with (graceful) smiles, bending waists, shaking breasts and fluttering skirts of their garments, ear-rings rocking against their cheeks, perspiring faces, and their braids and girdles loosened (on account of their swift movement) and celebrating the Lord in song, the aforesaid darlings of Sri Krsna shone brightly like flashes of lightning in a mass of clouds. Engaged in dancing an delighted with the touch of Sri Krsna, the Gopis - whose voice was sweetened with love, (nay), whose (sole) delight was loving devotion (to Sri Krsna) and whose music filled (the whole of) this universe-sang at the pitch of their voice.

This kind of Ras Leela (Divine romantic play) continues for years together. Many a people betraying their ignorance

are critical of the mystic way of working of Lord representing pinning of individual soul for the cosmic soul in term of human love and longing and call this a simple romance of a mortal for sexual pleasure. They fail to appreciate that thousands of Gopis, many of whom

were married while going to Shri Krishna for Ras Leela were never opposed by their husbands, even Radha's diligence with Sri Krishna was not one day affair but continued for years and

was the talk of the town, well known to her husband also. She feels herself free to join Lord Krishna at the call of him by playing on flute. In fact this is not ordinary romance but expression of spiritual love of individual soul for a cosmic soul represented by Shri Krishna. Lakhs of devotees of Shri Krishna still consider this act of life of the Lord as the most exuberated and unstinted with divine enjoyment and pleasure. The great sage Ved Vyasa who is the author of massive Puranas, 18 in numbers and Mahabharata, having over one lakh of Shlokas, would not get peace of mind till he wrote Srimad Bhagwat Purana sprouting him with spiritual love. The streets of Gokul and Vrindavan town where Shri Krishna played Raas Leela are still agog with recitation of Radhe-Radhey which has become a common way of greeting in that town.

Sant kabir a well known and celebrated saint of mediaeval India over whelmed with divine love of God uttered spontaneously " I am the beloved darling of Rama (the super power-God) ("Main hum Ram kii Bhuriya") (मैं हूं राम की बहुरियां)

Such being the case, the criticism and controversy attached to the Rasa-Leela with divine play of Lord Sri Krishna with Gopis is meaningless and speaks the ignorance of the philosophy behind the mystic way of the divine power.

Visualisation of Shri Krishna in cosmic form as the creator of universe mentioned in Bhagvad Gita 11.50

(H.T. 21st April, 2007)

EROTIC POSTURES AT TEMPLES

The fanciful and romantic posture depicted in the carvings have a close resemblance with the modern ones as seen in movies now a day.

Erotic carving in the various temples of Khazuraho and Konark, depict the various postures and ways of romance being followed in ancient India, proving that the important art of romance in ancient times was well developed and adults were not deprived of their share of entertainment.

WHY ROAMNTIC SCENCES ON OUT FRONT OF TEMPLES

Sex is a initial natural urge and manifests itself on getting adolescent in every human being. It is perhaps one of the richest sensation emanating from the union of two human bodies of opposite sex and according to an erotic scholar one can achieve the ultimate thereby. This natural urge is at the root of procreation of human race. Lord Krishna in Sri Mad Bhagat - Gita terms Sex 'Kama' as his Divinity (Vibhuti). It is perhaps this realization on the part of ancient's to have engrossed the romantic scenes on the out front of temples which are otherwise regarded as a holy place of worship of God.

KAMA SUTRA OF VATASYANA

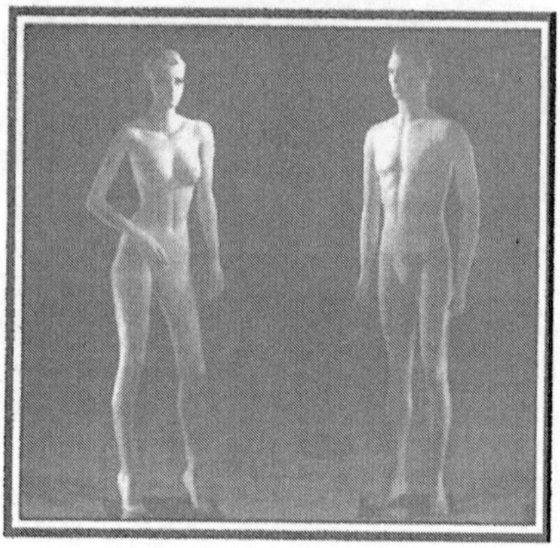

Vatasyana's Kama - Sutra is one of the most ancient works on sexology dating back to Pre-Christian Era. It is a standard treatise dealing systematically with the art of erotic with deep insight, bringing out the sensuous organs and erotic in female bodies. The Kama Sutra mainly dwells upon the following :

1. Categorization of man and woman according to sizes of their sexual organs and the urge in them.
2. Kisses pecks and bites.
3. Postures during inter course etc.

LOVE, ROMANCE AND KAM SUTRA

Love is the most powerful emotion felt since life involved and everything that has life feels it. For human being parents love, when we are young we yearn for friend's love and then

Kid's love, to share our little thoughts. Love has a way to everybody's heart and it can melt the hardest of heart. Just count of your heart beats in the first flash of love, isn't it beating faster? We do crazy things when we are in love and most of them are those that we would never dream of doing it otherwise. Don't you think that at times it overpowers you completely and you have no line of control.

Romance is the art of love, it may be without sex-motive or with sex motive. LEARNING of this art is very important for real joy. Vatasyana in his 'Kama - sutra' mentions sixty four skills that a man should acquire for joy. However, a modern guy at best knows four or five and he is always in a hurry for release. There is vast different between sex and romance. Sex is the mechanical process and just an avalanche of flesh and is a coarse one, whereas romance is an art of real pleasure and joy. One should understand the chemistry between the two consenting adults.

KISS, PECK AND KAM SUTRA

The new age has brought in a new culture called 'Kiss culture' which has become a way of greeting in high society - an expression of friendship and a warmer substitute of shaking hands which is normally a way of greeting between the people of same sex. It is a tender peck and a touch of lips against a Cheek or temple or the nose.

In Indian context a kiss is an expression of love and an act of out rage or a part of romance between willing couple.

Is kiss an Indian culture? The Kama Sutra of Vatasyna contains more than 200 references to different types of kisses not known to modernities and could well be taken as India's contribution in the field of erotic.

OLD AND NEW

Kama sutra mentions the different kinds of kisses during the sexual act and in fact the supplement to it, for maximising the enjoyment. However, in Modern context the kisses are mostly free from sex.

The Baburnam at the National Museum in New Delhi

KA

KISS KIS

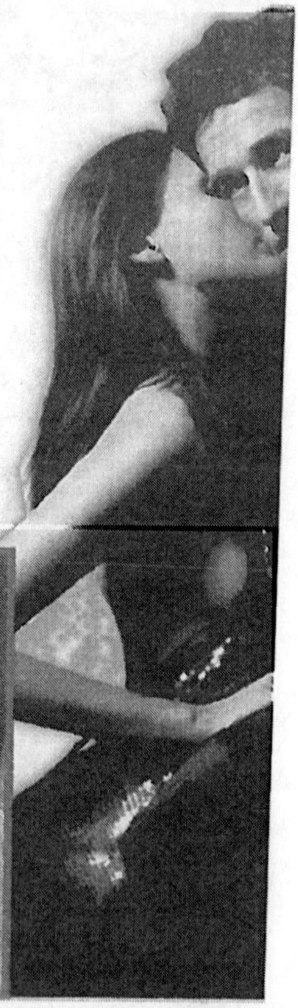

KIND

BUTTERFLY KISS

VACUUM KISS

CHOCOLATI

'RA

KISSES

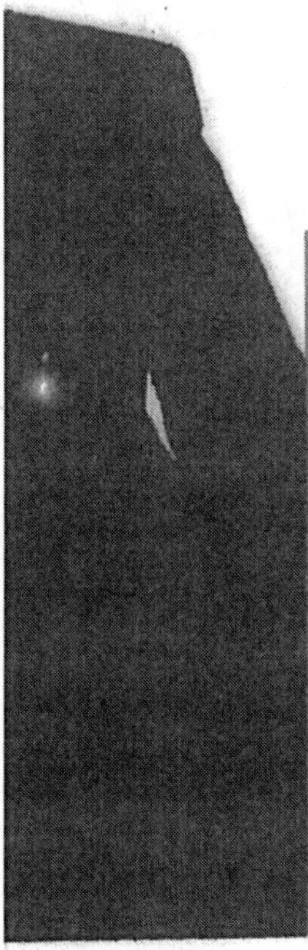

ISSES

K KISS FINGER KISS

CH KISS EYE KISS

TIGER KISS

KISS! WHERE?

Spot of Kiss Speaks a lot
Decipher its language

(In India)
I Love You

Kiss on Cheeks in Western world & in India have two different meaning

(In Western Culture)
I am your Friend

Remote Kissing
let us start loving

WHAT?

Kiss on Lips

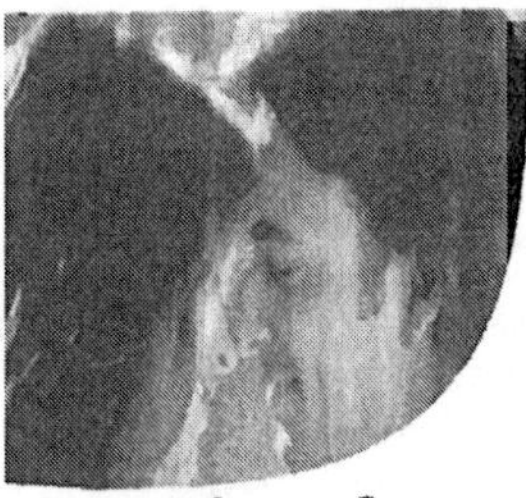

Kiss below the Check

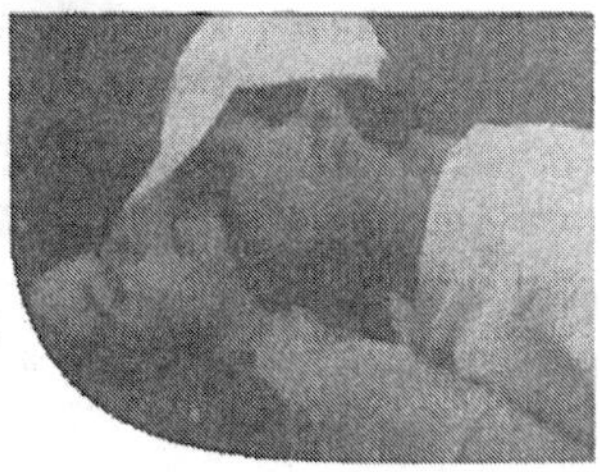

Let us have fun

I am in deep Love with you

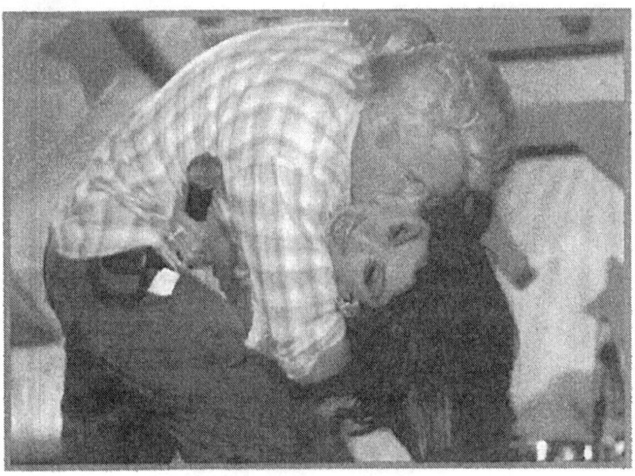

A Hot Kiss

REFERENCES

1. Srimad Bhagwad Gita, 6.15
2. Rig Veda X, 95.5
3. Ram Chrit Mansa - Bal Kanda Goswami Tulsi Das
4. रासोत्सवः सम्प्रवृत्तो गोपीमण्डलमण्डितः। योगेश्वरेण कृष्णेन तासां मध्ये द्वयोर्द्वयोः। प्रविष्टेन गृहीतानां कण्ठे स्वनिकटं स्त्रियः।3।
यं मन्येरन् नभस्तावद् विमानशतसङ्कुलम्। दिवौकसां सदाराणामौत्सुक्यापहृतात्मनाम्।4।
ततो दुन्दुभयो नेदुर्निपेतुः पुष्पवृष्टयः। जगुर्गन्धर्वपतयः सस्त्रीकास्तद्यशोऽमलम्।5।
वलयानां नूपुराणां किङ्किणीनां च योषिताम्। सप्रियाणामभूच्छब्दस्तुमुलो रासमण्डले।6।
तत्रातिशुशुभे ताभिर्भगवान् देवकीसुतः। मध्ये मणीनां हैमानां महामरकतो यथा।7।
पादन्यासैर्भुजविधुतिभिः सस्मितैर्भ्रूविलासैर्भज्यन्मध्यैश्चलकुचपटैः कुण्डलैर्गण्डलोलैः।
स्विद्यन्मुख्यः कबररशनाग्रन्थयः कृष्णवध्वो गायन्त्यस्तं तडित इव ता मेघचक्रे विरेजुः।8।
उच्चैर्जगुर्नृत्यमाना रक्तकण्ठ्यो रतिप्रियाः। कृष्णाभिमर्शमुदिता यद्गीतेनेदमावृतम्।9।
काचित् समं मुकुन्देन स्वरजातीरमिश्रिताः। उन्निन्ये पूजिता तेन प्रीयता साधु साध्विति। तदेव ध्रुवमुन्निन्ये तस्यै मानं च बह्वदात्।10।

- Srimad Bhagwad Purana, 33.3-10

9

Pre-marital and Extra Marital Relations in Ancient India

9

PRE-MARITAL AND EXTRA MARITAL RELATIONS IN ANCIENT INDIA

Kunti, the mother of Pandavas floating her new born baby (Karna) in river after putting him in a wooden box.

Pre-Marital relations have been condemned vehemently by our ancients since the age of Rigveda in strong terms. The whole philosophy of Hinduism is based upon the absolute virginity of a girl before her marriage and the mantras recited at the time of solmnising the marriage refer to the term of 'Kanya' means a virgin. This very consideration has been most important in prescribing the age of marriage for a girl by our preceptors and it was laid down that a girl must be married at her puberty age normally 11-12 years. Further, to rule out any chance of assault on the virginity of a girl, the age of marriage was brought down to 8 years during medieval India.

It was treated a worst stigma to a girl and to the entire family, if one was found to have pre marital relation of any kind.

This corroborates from the story given in Mahabharata about the birth of 'Karna' - a great warrior.

Kunti the mother of Pandvas, before her marriage had got a boon from a great sage. 'Durvasa', under the spell of which she was empowered to invoke a deity to bless her a son without under going sexual act. With a view to test the truthfulness of the boon, she worshipped and the Sun God, who appeared before her in divine form showered a boon and she thereby conceived and gave birth to a son. However this made her worried and hurried and in a bid to avoid stigma of pre-marital sex, she put the body in a wooden basket and floated in the nearby river which was later on captured by a charioteer. This child was named as 'Karana'.

With the passing of many a centuries, we have crossed over to a new age with complete transformation of mind and global environment. In metro cities casual sex is no big deal any more for young woman who want their share of fun before they settle down and casual sex is taken as simple as having a cup of coffee together. Young girls initiate casual encounter quite unabashedly according to a noted social psychiatrist. To the young women and guys, virginity is an over rated and out dated concept.

In Delhi, the capital city of India, many girls in their early twenties are finding it easy to have casual fling and they feel that it is the best time to have fun without commitment and casual sexual encounters with boys are really enjoyable. On the other hand, boys in their late-twenties feel happy to mingle with the new breed of bold and bedable women.

In India 'Living In Relationship' is now permitted by the Court of Law, where in a woman can live with his lover without marriage

Our Dharma Sutras and smrities are unanimous to condemn pre-marital sex in strong terms. According to Yajnavalkya (1.70, 72) an adulterous women should be deprived of her authority (over servants etc.), should be made to wear dirty cloths, should be given food just sufficient to enable her to live, should be treated with scorn and made to lie on the ground (not on a cot).

EXTRA MARITAL SEX

In Ancient India extra marital sex has been condemned by all Dharam sutras and smrities and was not permitted under any circumstances excerpt by 'Niyoga' a custom prevalent in early age of India.

Under the custom of - 'Niyoga' a woman was allowed to go to her brother-in-law or some other relation and could have conjugal relation with them for procreation[1] of children, in case, her husband had died or had been rendered incapable to procreate children particularly a son, who was considered necessary for salvation of mother and father. To die without son was regarded as a serious tragedy from financial, social and spiritual point of view. The number of sons to be raised by 'Niyoga' was restricted to three[2] but later on only one son was permitted and since there was a possibility of birth of a female child also as such the conjugal relations would continue for a long period.

In Mahabharta the three sons of Pandu-Yudhistra[3], Bhima and Arjuna were raised by 'Niyoga' as Pandu was rendered incapable to pro-create any male or female child under the spell of curse. Even the continuation of Kurn's dynastic was made possible by 'Niyoga' and Maharishi Vedvyas a was called upon by his mother Satyawati for seeding[4] after the death of Vichitra Viriya, leaving behind two wives as widow having no son.

In Ancient India it was very difficult for a young woman to pass her life without livelihood and having no children. A regular re-marriage was also not easy and under the circumstances 'Niyoga' system was invoked to help the unfortunate woman

Fig. 2

which appears strange and unrespectable in the modern period. This system of'Niyoga' which was opposed by many preceptors and also by Manu, was discontinued in due course.

It was felt that the Niyoga commits a gross violation of conjugal fidelity and is also against the sacred vows taken by the wife before the holy Fire God for strict fidelity. Even puranas condemned this system with the result that after 600 A.D. the 'Niyoga' system lost its steam and went out of vogue.

SEX AND SAGES OF ANCIENT INDIA

In spite of the repeated directions provided by 'Dharm sutras' the fact remains that the sex is a natural urge which sometime upsurges so strongly that it is difficult to resist it and people lose control and fail to restrain themselves and it is no wonder that sages and hermits who have renounced the world and have devoted themselves to meditation and spiritual activities sometimes get astray and lose control to yield to his sexual urge. Lord Krishna in Bhagvad Gita has admitted that 'manah'[5] of a person is fragile and very difficult to be controlled and only the practice with total renunciation one can have some control.

Shiva Purana mentions that the God of Sex-kama Deva when tried to invade lord shiva to seduce him from the path of austerity by arousing the feeling of kama. the lord had to resort

Lord Shiva opens his third eye to burn down Kama

to open his third eye by using his super power to kill down 'Kama Deva' – the God of sex. This shows the strong pull and force of the sexual urge in a human being.

Such being the case many our sages, leading a life of Tapas and Yoga in hermitage far from the dazzle of cities were over -powered by sex as given under.

A visualisation of Puranic nymph

Guru Dhrona Charya :- A famous figure of 'Mahabharta' and the teacher of Pandva and Kaurva in Dhanur Vidya owes his birth to the irresistible sexual urge on the part of saga Bhardavaja mentioned as his father when he saw a nymp of unparalleled beauty in semi-clad sari standing on the bank of river Ganga.

Kripa Chariya :- The birth story of Kripa Charya - a known figure of Mahabharta and appointed as a teacher for archery of Pandvas and Kauravas, is also a similar one. His father saint 'Shardy Wana', when he was undergoing penance, saw a nymph of matchless beauty twisting with romantic exposure before him making the saint lose control on his sexual passion.

The birth of Ravana is again based up on a similar story according to which Ravana was conceived by his mother Kalkashi, who accosted sage 'Vashrava'.

REFERENCES :

1. कुलाय हि स्त्री दीयते इति उपदिशन्ति अन्यजातमस्ति।
   - G.D.S.-I
2. नातश्चतुर्थ प्रसवमापत्स्वपि वदन्त्युत।
   अतः परं स्वैरिणी स्याद्बन्धकी पञ्चमे भवेत्।।
   - Mahabharta 132, 63-4
3. Mahabharta. Ch.3.
4. Mahabharta Ch.3.
5. Srimad Bhagwad Gita 6.35.

10

Divorce & Remarriage in Ancient India

10

DIVORCE & REMARRIAGE IN ANCIENT INDIA

'Oh lady! get up, come back to the world of living; you are lying by the side of a dead person. Thy wife hood to me, who has siezed thy hand, is now-commenced.'

- Rig Veda. X.18,8

Divorce is a common affair in the western countries. Thanks to the liberalized provisions of act of law that divorce takes place on filmsy grounds which has resulted in a situation that both of the spouses feel insecure after marriage for a long period of time. In case of illness either of the spouse would get herself/himself hospitalized rather lying sick at home to avoid irritation to the other partner.

The mental agony caused to a kid of 4-5 years of age who craves for the affection of mother and father both could be well imagined in the event of divorce and thereby forced separation from mother or father and it is no surprise that multi-thousands of kids suffer from mental disorder and psychological aliments. Under Islamic religion divorce is supposed to be so easy that simply by uttering Talaque, Talaque, Talaque by the husband will tentamount to divorce though the other partner may not be willing for the same.

In modern India the law does not encourage divorce though the same is allowed in some genuine cases. As regards ancient India, under the marriage ritual called 'satpadi' where in bride and groom tied with nuptial knot take seven steps together, and exchange vows – commitments with fire God as witness for remaining perpetually associated with each other in all stages and circumstances, make the marriage relation as permanent and unbreakable.

The in depth study of ancient literature, however, reveals that resort to divorce has been made under some rare cases as under:

MENTAL DIVORCE BY LORD SHIVA (An Ideal form of Divorce) :

Ramayana mentions the story of mental divorce by Lord Shiva on having come to know disguising of his consort Sati as Sita to test the divinity of Shri Rama who was worshipped as his God by Lord Shiva, as such Sita was beholden as reverent mother. Once Sati disguised herself as Sita, she was not acceptable as his wife by Lord Shiva and he, therefore, divorced her mentally and absorbed himself in deep meditation for months. Sati, thereafter went to her parents' home to participate in a Yajna ceremony being organized by her father to celebrate his appointment as 'Daksha Prajapati' and on seeing the disrespect shown to Lord Shiva who was still be holden as husband, she could not tolerate this insult to her husband and jumped and burnt herself in fire altar. She took rebirth as Parvati, the daughter of Himalaya and practiced strict penance to marry Lord Shiva who finally agreed to marry her and a grand marriage was held again between Parvati and Lord Shiva.

ABANDONMENT AMOUNTING TO DIVORCE BY SHRI RAMA :

Shri Rama after his coronation as King of Ayodhya on return from his 14 years' exile in forest was reported by his spy about adverse reaction of a section of people against retaining Sita as his wife, though she remained in captivity of Ravana for one year and her fidelity was doubtful. Shri Rama being the ideal King and being particular to the criticism by his people, got abandoned Sita in forest through his younger brother Laxmana.

Sita, thereafter, took shelter in the Ashrama of Rishi Valmiki but she would regard Shri Rama as her husband. This was very clear from the fact that Sita stopped fighting her twin sons

Lav & Kush with Lord Rama, who escorted by his army, came to get the sacrificial horse released from the custody of Lav & Kusha. Thereafter, at the call of Lord Rama, she went to Ayodhya also where Ashwamedh Yajna was being performed.

PROVISIONS OF DIVORCE IN DHARMA SUTRAS

From the above it need not infer that it was open to men only to abandon or divorce their wives on certain grounds. Dharmshastras made the provisions for abadonment or divorce by woman also. A hymn of Rig-Veda[1] exorts a widow to marry again and live happily. Athraveda[2] contains a reference regarding a woman for re-marriage, perhaps on divorce of her living husband. Manu – the Hindu lawgiver, mentions that a husband who is insane or suffering from an incurable and serious communicable disease, there is nothing wrong to abandon such husband which amounts to the divorce (Manusmriti IX-79)[3]. Further Dharmasutras are unanimous on the point that if a husband has gone on long journey and not returned for 5 years or so, the wife can unite herself and remarry a second person.[4]

Parasara – a preceptor of post Vedic times[5] also allows remarriage by a woman if her husband is impotent and boycotted by the society while other preceptors, prescribe a long period of waiting which varies from 1-8 years for different cases. Kunling makes divorce rules still more liberal and allows divorce even if a man apprehends danger from his wife or vice-versa or the husband and wife hate each other. These provisions, however, were made for only Asuras, Gandharvas, Rakshasa and Paisacha forms of marriage only.

Buddhist literature e.g. Dhammapada, Majhima, Nikaya etc. mention certain cases of divorce where woman contracted the second marriage after having come to know that her husband has married the second wife. There are cases where nuns made several divorces one after the other.

From the above an impression goes that there have been frequent cases of divorce in ancient India. The fact remains that whereas, in lower sections of society, there were many cases of divorce between man and woman, however, in general, the divorce and remarriage cases were almost negligible after 1200 A.D.

While marriage by and large is regarded as permanent and undisolvable with the high ideals of marriage, it is possible only if the husband and wife are prepared to make great sacrifices and be accomodative and divorce should only be treated as the last resort.

It is heartening that 'Hindu Marriage and Divorce Act' passed by the Parliament now allows divorce if there is desertion for 5 years. Impotency or idiotic. Communicable or vulnerable diseases are also the sufficient grounds for divorce. The Act further provides divorce in case of cruelity, or where the change of religion of husband or wife.

REFERENCES :

1. Rigveda X. 18.8
2. Athrvaveda - IX.S. 27-8
3. उन्मत्तं पतितं क्लीबमबीजं पापरोगिणम्। - Manu Smriti IX.79
4. Vashisht Dharma Sutra XVII.67
5. नष्टे मृते प्रव्रजिते क्लीबे च पतिते पतौ।
   पञ्चवापत्सु नारीणां पतिरन्यो विधीयते।। - Parasara IV.24